THE MEDITATION BIBLE

With Audio Tutorials LINK

Also by Richard P. Matthews

THE MEDITATION BIBLE

With Audio Tutorials LINK

Richard P. Matthews

Revitalizing In-sight®
Hill, New Hampshire

PUBLISHED BY REVITALIZING IN-SIGHT®
Copyright © 2017 by Richard P. Matthews
This book is a Divinely inspired spiritual revelation. All the visions recorded here are those given to the author by the 'Great I Am.' Bible translations are translations of the author.
Published in the United States by Revitalizing In-sight®,
Hill, New Hampshire.
www.RevitalizingIn-sight.com
The portrayal of the symbol ⊙ is a registered trademark of Wicke Unlimited.
Library of Congress Control Number:
2007932585
Cataloging Data.
Matthews, Richard P.
The Meditation Bible/Richard P. Matthews —
1st ed. p. cm.
1. THE MEDITATION BIBLE—Meditation. 2. Spiritual Teachings 3. Inspirational 4. Body-mind-spirit-earth 5. New Life 6. The Great I Am
I. Title. II. Matthews, Richard P.
ISBN: 978-0-9798106-7-1
PRINTED IN THE UNITED STATES OF AMERICA
10 8 6 4 2 0 1 3 5 7 9
First Edition

ACCLAIM

CONTENTS

INTRODUCTION

"Moses said to God, 'What do I say your name is?'
God said, 'I-am- האיה *-I-am.'"*
(Exodus 3:13b-14a)

The quote above is what started me on my journey. In this verse, our creator is telling us not only who 'I am' is but where 'I am' is, **within us** and in **all things**. The Hebrew word האיה (Heb. hayah) means "dynamic essence" or "essence of being." That is why in the early Hebrew church the word God was forbidden. They called their Deity the 'I am' or the 'Great I am.' My Spirit churned within me as the meaning of this word flowed through my body. Through meditation, I soon found the 'Great I Am' within me and connected.

This book creates a clear path for the spiritual seeker to get to their inner essence, spiritual center, or as 'I am' calls it, our 'Great I Am' center. This path has four steps. Firstly, we need to be clearly aware of who we are seeking, why we need to connect with 'I am', and what we must do to prepare for our "Spiritual Journey."

Next, we need to learn to listen to our body and go inside to experience our inner being. Thirdly, we need to discover our source of breath, which can help us to block the chattering rational thoughts and ego. Finally, we need to connect with the 'Great I Am' within us and accept 'I am's purpose for our lives. That will be the beginning of your journey.

1- The Spiritual Journey

Spirituality is in our DNA. We all experience the yearning for something deeper than the routines of our everyday lives. Many modern scientists now realize that there is a higher intelligence at work in the universe. The order and complexity of the DNA of a single cell would fill eight large volumes. The body of knowledge available to every man, woman, and child is almost beyond human comprehension. Our knowledge has positively changed the quality and ease of our lives forever. Yet in the area of spirituality our knowledge has created a quagmire of conflicting thoughts and violent disagreements. Underneath all that knowledge we sense that there must be something else.

Lao Tzu says:
On the way to knowledge
Many things are accumulated.
On the way to wisdom
Many things are discarded.
Less and less effort is used
Until things arrange themselves.

Instinctively in our DNA, we are
feeling that this deeper identity lies within
us, where everything "arranges itself."
That feeling leads us on a spiritual
journey.

The need to find that deeper identity
causes every spiritual seeker to ponder the
questions; Who am I? Why am I here?
What is my purpose in life? These
spiritual questions reveal the desire to
connect with our essence of being, our
inner being. For many millennia that
longing has driven people to one religious
practice or another. A few religious
leaders say they have connected, but then
never unlock the door for others. Joshua
spoke about this regarding the religious
leaders in his time, and it has been a
problem ever since. Martin Buber writes,
"Nothing hides the face of God from us
better than organized religion does."
(BETWEEN MAN AND MAN, 1947)

So, what are they hiding?

The big secret is, the 'Great I am' is inside you. The 'Great I am' is not something outside us, above us, or beyond us, but the 'Great I am' is in our spiritual center, our inner being. 'I am' is the "essence of being" in us. 'I am' is our 'Great I Am' center. Hear these words, "The kingdom of God is in you." "Heaven is in you." "I am in the Father and the Father is in me." "I am in you, and you are in me." "You are sons (and daughters) of the living God." "You are one with God." All these are phrases which appear all throughout the sacred texts repeatedly.

We need to let the 'Great I am' reveal the 'I am' presence in our inner being. The intent and goal of the creator is to be part of our everyday lives. Our goal and longing is to find and make the 'Great I am' a part of our everyday lives. Yes, we want the same thing, and that should be no surprise. After all, we are one. So, the answer to all our spiritual questions is in our spiritual center, our 'Great I Am' center. 'I am' has a purpose for everyone's life. Our journey is taking us there, and we must be ready to accept 'I am's purpose for us.

2- Listening to the Body

Your body is literally your Temple. It is not a place where you go. It is the place where you are right NOW. Your body is talking to you all the time. But, are you listening? Shure, you know about your five senses: sight, hearing, touch, taste, and smell. However, do you know you have a sixth sense. All living creatures on the planet have it, but humans are ignoring it.

Our sixth sense is **awareness**. To find it again you must learn to listen to your body. You must become an observer of your body. You need to go inside your body and listen to what it is saying to you. It does not use words, but it uses a level of feelings that will make you aware of what it is saying to you. It is a universal language in all humans. Unlike your rational thought, your awareness will never lie to you. You can absolutely trust everything it is telling you.

On this step, you will start to learn how to shut down your chattering rational thoughts and ego. This is important, if you are to discover the depths of your inner body.

Below and on the audio disk, I will take you through the process of discovering your inner body. This is essential for this meditation process.

3- Discovering Your Natural Breathing

There are many things the body does all on its own. One of them is breathing. Yet, have you discovered your source of breath? Probable not. Your rational thoughts and ego do not want you to find it. So, someone tells you to take a deep breath, and you puff out your chest and assume you are taking a deep breath. Your rational thought tells you, you took a deep breath, and your ego tells you, you look fantastic. When in reality, you barely took a sip of air.

However, every night when you go to bed, your body breaths naturally. You need to rediscover that breathing process. Because, it will help you to block your chattering rational thoughts and ego. It will also help you find the 'Great I Am' within your **inner being** and enable you to hear 'I am's voice with your awareness.

Below and on the audio disk, I will guide you through this important step. This meditation process will take you deep into the **inner center** of your body and open you up to the Love-light of the 'Great I am.'

4- A Map to Your 'Great I Am' Center

The goal of this meditation process is to connect with the 'Great I Am' within your inner being and accept 'I am's purpose for your life. That is a true Free Will choice.

The Buddha in his early meditation focused on the eight-fold path, which he thought would lead to a higher intelligence. He then continued to go deeper and found nirvana, a peaceful blackness, which he described as absolute nothingness. In nirvana, all rational thought and the ego no longer exist. Finally, in his meditation he discovers that the absolute nothingness contains absolutely everything. In it he finds the Love-light of the 'Great I Am' within his inner being.

When we reach our 'Great I Am' center through this meditation process, a portal opens and the Love-light of the 'Great I Am' pours into us.

In Matthew 6:6 Joshua describes meditation, "Here's what I want you to do: Find a quiet, secluded place so you won't be tempted to role-play before the 'Great I Am' within you. Just be there as simply and honestly as you can manage. The focus will shift from you to the 'Great I Am' within you, and you will experience 'I am's Love-light."

While meditating, you will learn to shut down your chattering rational thoughts and ego so you can get to your 'Great I Am' center, and embrace 'I am' and let 'I am' embrace you. Those who get there discover the greatest Love-light they will ever know.

Every day, I awaken to the Love-light within me. 'I am' greats me and guides me through the day. With constant meditation, sometimes lasting less than a few seconds, we remain connected all day. In moments of crisis, the 'Great I am' is always right here within me to help me through any difficulty. 'I am's presence keeps me present.

Below and on the audio disk, I will help you make that connection to the 'Great I Am' within you. I will even help you see more clearly your Free Will choice. However, only you can make that choice.

So how do we begin this journey? The 'Great I Am' wants you to be aware of what happened in the beginning, which now makes this journey so difficult for us. So, let's begin at the beginning. We need to know how all our distractions started so we can get past them.

Like all the above, the words I write here are 'I am's words. I am simply taking dictation.

CHAPTER 1

Before Creation

I ask the 'Great I Am' within me, "Why don't you destroy evil? You have the power."

"Yes, I do. I can, but I won't."

"I don't understand."

The 'Great I Am's hand is over my heart. "I need to show you the beginning. Close your eyes and do your meditation. Tell me what you see."

I close my eyes.

After a moment, "There is only darkness and an empty space. It feels peaceful with a profound silence.

"There is nothing.

"Now I see a glowing blue sphere flowing through the vast empty space. You are the sphere.

"There is an energy swirling within the blue sphere. That energy is your mind. You have an image of everything you want to create. There are so many; they are beyond my calculation. I can feel they are all very dear to you.

"You know them in every detail, every cell, every atom and every electron particle. I feel your connection with them all. But they are in your mind and cannot emerge.

"Now I feel your longing to bring it all into being. Oh my, your longing is so great. It is almost too great to bear.

"Now I see your blue sphere moving off through the vast empty space. The space seems endless and void of all life. I wait and wait. Then I realize there is no time.

"Now I see another glowing red sphere floating through the darkness. It has a regular pulsing rhythm within it, like a beating heart.

"It too has an energy that is flowing out from its center.

"I feel it faintly as it comes closer.

"Now I feel it all around me and within me. It is the most powerful Love that I have ever felt.

"But I am not the one; She does not feel my presence as She floats on into empty space.

"Now I feel Her longing as She floats off to find the right One. Her longing feels even greater than yours does, and I realize that you are Her One.

"How will you ever find each other in the vastness of this space?

"Now after time without number or quicker than the present moment passes into the next moment, I see the two spheres moving toward each other. They flow and float. They float and flow ever closer.

"Slowly and slower, they come together until they are all but touching. Their longing fades away as they look deeply into each other.

"The red sphere surrounds the blue sphere with Her Love. She looks within the blue sphere and sees all the images waiting to come into being. She sees the crystal city in its splendor.

"The blue sphere releases the energy of its mind and engulfs the red sphere. 'I am' looks within the red sphere and sees Her beating heart pumping life through countless veins. 'I am' sees within them the red fluid, in which She is pumping all Her life giving power.

"The love of the red sphere penetrates the blue sphere and surrounds every image in the mind of the 'Great I Am.'

"The energy of the 'Great I Am's' mind penetrates the red sphere and charges the blood within Her heart and veins with 'I am's Light.

"Now they touch. Now they press closer together distorting the outer shape of their spheres."

Suddenly, I realize and cry out, "She is the Divine Mother!"

As I say those words, "I see a brilliant flash of **LIGHT** and hear a voice say the Word 'LIGHT.'

"Then, I hear an enormous **BANG!** I feel the flesh on my face which is forcing my skin back tightly. My whole body is throbbing from the percussion. My closed eyes watch the white-hot light grow brighter. Then, the shock wave passes.

"I open my eyes and see the two spheres become ONE, swirling and pulsing together. The sphere is bigger and a dazzling white. All this is happening in the same present moment.

"The ONE brilliant white sphere is spinning so fast that specs of light are cast in all directions. Out of the ONE brilliant white light emerges a transparent female human form. She is beautiful with long flowing hair.

"The Divine Mother is talking to you. You have a transparent human male form. Your facial features are African, as it was when I first saw you when I was twelve. Your body is muscular.

"As the two of you speak, stars of many different shapes come out of your mouths. I cannot understand your star language.

"While you are talking to each other, I see what looks like a ribbon of mist and light that is flowing and floating around, between and through the Divine Mother and you.

"Yes, I can see it now. He is your son. I can see His face in the ribbon of light, but His body has no form. Now, I hear His voice.

"He translates your star language for me. I hear you and the Divine Mother planning creation. Then there is a deep silence and stillness.

"In the next moment or time without number...

"I hear and see the voice from the ribbon of Light Wording all things into being, the Divine Mother fills them with Love. Slowly, everything takes shape behind Her. The stars, the planets, our world takes shape and comes into being.

"Now, quicker than the present moment passes into the next present moment or after time without number, all the images that are in your mind are worded into being and are given love and life fluid by the Divine Mother.

"Through the images in your Mind,

the Wording of them, and the Devine Mother's Love you three make all things, and all things come into being.

"I can feel the combined energy of the Three flowing out through the universe. Their feeling is unity, harmony, oneness, peace and joy. From the voices of everything in creation, I can hear them singing their praises to the creator Three. Your combined Light fills everything as they connect with you in their 'Great I Am' center.

In the next present moment or after time without number, I see you, the Wording Light and the Divine Mother hovering over Adam and Eve. The Word is putting them together from the inside out. The Devine Mother is filling them with Love and their life's blood. Then you fill them with your Light, your presence and breathe life into them; your breath to them; their breath to you.

"Now as the 'Great I am' within, you say to them, 'I want you to have Free Will. It is an important part of who **we** are. It will make it easy for you to find Me within your Inner Being. It will make it easier for you to Love us and each other. It gives you the choice to walk with Me or not. Because the choice is yours, it will make our connection stronger. By connecting to Me you will be connecting to everything else on the planet. You will see all things as I see them. You will communicate with all things as I do, and they will know you as they know Me. You will be able to help them maintain the harmony in all creation.'

"That is the life that Adam and Eve received from you three. This is their reality, and through you, they are aware of everything."

I look at the 'Great I Am' assuming 'I am' finished.

'I am' says, with a hand still on my heart, "Keep meditating. You need to know the rest."

I go back into my meditation, "I see that the newness is gone. The earth is buzzing with life.

"Again, I see you and the Divine Mother speaking in your star language, only now I can see that she is in a rage. Her tone is harsh and shrill. Your Word Light translates everything for me.

"The Divine Mother says to you, 'I want you to give me the power to create on my own.'

"You reply, 'I cannot do that.'

"'Why not? You gave that power to

Eve.'

"'That was different. Besides, she can only create from the seed of Adam.'

"The Divine Mother is growing angry, 'How is that different?'

"'They are not creating out of nothing.'

"'I demand that you give me the power. Why should you keep the power all to yourself?'

"'I am not keeping it to myself. Creation is from the three of us.'

"She is becoming furious, 'I don't believe you! Give me the power!'

"You are patient and gentle, 'How can I give you what I do not have? Creation could only happen when **We** became **One**.'

"She is in a full rage now, 'You are hiding it from me! Give it to me!'

"'I am not hiding anything. When we met, I was wandering through the darkness of space. All my images were locked inside me. It was you and our Son, who unlocked them. He worded them into being, your Love filled them and I breathed life into them. We can only create as three together.'

"She is not listening to any of this. In a flash, Her love flips into hate, 'Then let me go down to earth, and give me dominion over everything there. At least I can have power over that creation! Do not refuse me!'

"'Go then,' you say. 'But you shall not destroy our creation, and you shall not destroy those who connect with me. When you see your mistake, come back.'

"She says, 'I agree! Do you agree?'

"You sigh and say, 'I agree. The Love you brought to me and taught me shall always be here for you.'

"Now I see a new image emerge from under the Divine Mother's feet. It is like smoke from a fire. As she laughs a hideous laugh, it curls up around her and takes shape behind her. It is the image of a dragon, with huge wings.

"Slowly she becomes a red dragon with powerful wings. She can change her shape at will. As she flies up and circles us, she screeches back at you and your Son, 'You are both fools! With very little encouragement from me, your precious puny humans will destroy your creation and each other! Hssssss, hssssss, Hssssss!' she hisses as she flies down to Earth. I cannot see the place.

"Then I see Lucifer, one of your archangels who helped you in creation, leaving with her. Now, I hear you saying to your Son, 'I cannot see where all this is going. What part did Lucifer play in all this? I sense her anger and hatred, which I never saw before, because they are not in Me.'"

I look into the face of the 'Great I Am'. There are tears running down 'I am's cheeks. I ask, "You still love her, don't you?"

"Yes. Can you see why I can't destroy her?"

"Of course." Then I add hesitantly, "But I should tell you that I have seen the Dragon Lady many times in my meditation. I quickly learned that only Love will chase her away."

"I know. But what you don't know is that if enough people can reflect the Love back on her, she may come home. And then creation can continue. The Love has to come from the in-lightened spirit within the people, not from me."

CHAPTER 2
In the Beginning

The 'Great I Am' says to me, "Listen, really listen, listen with every fiber of your being."

'I am' comes to me while I am sitting in my morning meditation. 'I am' often just starts to talk to me. Only now, 'I am's urgency fills every fiber of my inner being.

"You saw what happened with the Devine Mother. But now, you must see what she did. This is My story, with **human kind**, from the beginning. Listen and know how **we** got in this mess. Yes '**we**', for I am part of the mess, just as I am part of you and all things. Listen, so we can untie this knot that binds all creation."

'I am's Love-light glows within my body. I am listening with all the awareness that is in me. The 'Great I Am' is filling me with a clear image of Adam and Eve and all things created by the Three.

'I am' reminds me, "As you saw in the beginning, We gave all creation 'Free Will' to follow the order of the universe. It is a great thing, and all is in balance.

Then, as I explained before, the Devine Mother of creation, the woman you like to call the 'Dragon Lady', comes to Me wanting the power of creation for herself.

"I would gladly give it, but creation is of Us Three. The images are in My mind. When I find Her Love, our Son is born. Then My beloved Son words My images into being. With Her Love, She fills all things with their life fluid and Love, and I breathe life into them. We Three are in all things, with all things, the inner Being of all things, the Love-light of all things.

"As you saw, Her Love flips 180 degrees, because she is unable to see through her hatred that the power is in Us Three. She leaves in a rage, and her hideous laughter makes the universe shutter."

I sense a sadness as 'I am' recalls these moments again. There is no anger. There is only an urgency for someone to listen and comprehend what is happening.

"Let us set the record straight. Adam and Eve are the object of her first devastating act of defiance and destruction. I sense, she does not like that I give them so much attention.

"Adam and Eve are both connected

with Me and fulfilling their life's purpose with joy and satisfaction. They listen and follow my guidance. They are in total harmony with all of creation.

"They know real Love for each other. Their Love relationship is rooted in each other's connection to Me within them. It creates a deep feeling of oneness, a deep awareness of each other's needs and desires. Their lives become totally entwined.

"Their Love produces **five** endearing qualities between them. Their **communication** is based on a complete understanding of their partner. They develop a total **acceptance** of who their partner is. With their connection to me, their lovemaking develops an intimate **inner awareness** of their partner's needs and passionate craving at each moment. They each develop a **willingness** to put the satisfaction and fulfillment of their partner first. Their experience of pleasure and **unity** is so powerful; it fills Me with joy. More than once, I say to Myself, 'This is how Love should be.'

"In all respects they are totally equal. They speak and communicate with all living creatures, plants and rocks on the planet. They know all their languages, all

their needs and their connections to Me.
They are all part of the order of the
universe and living in total harmony.

"Into that bliss, the Dragon Lady (as
you like to call her) slithers in to reap
havoc with the planet. The Dragon
Lady's hatred is about to change all those
positive feelings. She has a plan. She tries
to give it to all the creatures and things on
the planet, but she fails with every other
living creature, plant and rock on the
planet. They want nothing to do with it.

"But, she realizes how to gain control
over the earth, by gaining control over
humanity. She calculates exactly what to
do and how to do it, so humanity will
destroy the planet for her.

"The Dragon Lady comes up with
the idea of how to plant deductive
reasoning in the left brain of Adam and
Eve. This would be a corrupt logic, and
give her control over the human rational
thoughts as long as she can make it
dominant over inductive logic in the
rational mind.

"With this plan, she comes to Adam
and Eve to offer them a bargain. She
approaches Adam first."

I interrupt the 'Great I Am, "What?
I was under the understanding that Eve

was first, and she tempted Adam."

"That is the way it ended up in the oral tradition," 'I am' explains. "However, there is one major clue that remains that tells you Adam was first to buy into the bargain, not Eve. Adam was the first to say, 'She made me do it.' He was already using his rational thought to justify his actions and pass the blame.

"This is how the Dragon Lady sold her bargain. She said to Adam, 'I will show you how to find the great power of your rational thought, which is the same power of the I Am in creation.' Note the lie here, because in my mind the idea of all things was simply present in every detail. It is not a product of rational thought. In fact, to me rational thought is useless. My conclusions do not need proof or justification.

"She continues to sell her deal, 'You have the power to create things on your own, without 'I am's assistance.' This is lie number two, not even she can create on her own.

"Here comes lie number three, 'You will have absolute power over everything on the planet. It will be your dominion and under your control, to do with as you please.' Everything is in harmony with each other. She wants to destroy that harmony. She wants Adam to believe this is 'Free Will,' but it is only a rational choice or freedom of will. Rational choice and freedom of will only bind humans to her negativity.

"Eve could see right through her. 'What is the value of all this?' She questioned the Dragon Lady, "Why should we want this 'rational thought' thingy? We already have everything we need. It seems like a total waste of energy.'

"The Dragon Lady sweetens the deal, 'If you accept my bargain and embrace your rational thought, I will throw in a bonus. I will give you an ego. This precious gift will help you apricate everything you gain and want to gain more. It will help you to be the best that you can be, better than anyone or anything else, better than the I Am.'

"Adam starts coaxing Eve, 'Come on dear, what's the harm in it? Try and be more positive. Let's give it a try.'

"Eve is defensive, 'I am positive. Everything is positive. Why should I risk changing that for some silly old 'rational thought' and an 'ego'?'

"The Dragon Lady smiles and warms

up to Eve, 'Look my dear, I will give you your ego first so you can see what a difference it makes.' She touches her forehead. 'There you are! Come here and look in the pool of water. See how lovely you are.'

"Eve is not buying it, 'I am beautiful. It can't make me more beautiful?'

"'Yes dear, you will be the most beautiful!' The Dragon Lady grins.

"Eve looks in the pool. She turns to see herself from all angles. Her eyes light up and a broad smile appears on her face, 'I am more beautiful! My figure is the best I have ever seen it. But I have to do something with my hair.'

"Eve turns to Adam, 'OK Adam. We can do it for a little while."

"Everything she tells them is either a half-truth or a lie, but I never prepared them for falsehood. She says to them, 'The Ego is the most important companion to the human rational thoughts. It will help you realize your superiority to all other things. With it, you will see your own greatness. It will drive you to succeed or win at all coast. With it, you will not just want more, you will want the most, you will want the best and you will know you are entitled to it.'

"Next, the Dragon Lady goes to work on their rational thoughts. Although, the early scholars come up with the metaphor of a tree of 'Truth and Knowledge' and an apple as a 'forbidden fruit', the image and meaning is misleading. There is no such tree, and Adam and Eve already have Truth and Knowledge in their brains, because they connect with Me.

"What the Dragon Lady does is draw them away from the Truth, to focus their attention on their rational thought and supposed superior knowledge to the rest of creation. Adam jumps at the chance, and his new Ego has him chasing after the idea of superior knowledge.

"Ultimately, Eve becomes sold. She starts to think of herself as supper intelligence.

"That is when the Dragon Lady comes up with the BIG Lie. She says, 'How would you like to know the secret about creation. Believe me, I know that from firsthand experience.'

"Eve asks the Dragon Lady, 'Are you saying that you can show us how to create?'

"She turns on the charm, saying, 'I sure can! It is simple. (Here it comes; the Great Miss-direction.) All you have to do is listen to what your rational thought is telling you. (Now, she supports her case by playing to their Ego.) It is all-powerful. Your thought is superior to all others. In fact, no other species or thing can think like you. Your thinking is the definition of intelligence. All other intelligence is inferior to yours. (Finally she confirms the LIE.) Listen to your rational thought; it will never lie to you.'

"That is how this MESS begins. When the human species listens only to their rational brain chatter, they cannot listen to Me in their inner Being. They are not able to connect with Me and share in all that I can give them.

"The moment Adam and Eve begin to listen to their rational brain chatter, they cut themselves off from Me. I do not cast them out of Eden. I am right there within them. They left Eden to find what they lost. Their real Love-light connection becomes a dream, a fantasy, a myth. They lost their **five** endearing qualities of Love. They replaced Love with an idea of love, which is nothing more than sexual passion.

"They can no longer communicate with the animals, birds, creatures, plants and rocks. They can no longer feel and sense the harmony in the universe. In fact, everything their rational brain chatter is telling them is a total disruption of that harmony. Their rational brain chatter is telling them they have only five senses, when they have six. The rest of the planet knows that, but not humans.

"I deeply love their sons, Cain and Able, and they both connect to me as children. This gives Me great hope. Then as they come into adulthood, their rational brain chatter begins. I struggle to help Cain shut down his ego, but in an instant his rational brain chatter transforms into brain clutter and then into brain chaos. He totally moves to his **Dark Side**, which is a mental state created by rational thoughts.

"Cain becomes consumed by his anger and hatred. The same anger and hatred I experienced in the Dragon Lady. In the next instant, he kills his brother, Able. There is only one thing more destructive than rational brain chatter, brain clutter and brain chaos, and that is brain deception."

I am aware that the 'Great I Am' is feeling a deep remorse, like a parent losing their own child. Then it hits me, of course, Cain and Able, are 'I am's first-born.

I can't resist asking, "Have you ever regretted giving us the gift of real "Free Will?"

Setting sadness aside, 'I am' responds, "No! It was and still is what I intended it to be. However, I had no idea that your 'Dragon Lady' could and would come up with the corrupting 'rational thought and ego,' which she gave to Adam and Eve. That gift became their bondage and produced their falsely perceived freedom of will.

"Your real "Free Will' allows you to choose to live with Me within you, or to turn away from Me and rely totally on your rational thoughts. With the real "Free Will," there is no absolute obedience required. You make your choice in every minute of every day.

"On the other hand, the false freedom of will is a condition set up by the rational thoughts which gives you a choice between obeying or not obeying a set of laws, which you make. Thus, your ethical choices are but an illusion. With the falsely perceived freedom of will, absolute obedience to the law is mandatory and to break the law will result

in severe punishment. This makes the
false freedom of will no Free Will at all.
Here is how it happened."

'I am' pauses for a moment, then
asks, "How would you like to hear it first
hand from Adam and Eve? Now they are
right here with me again. I feel they
would enjoy telling their own story."

Within a moment, I feel Adam and
Eve's presence. I ask Adam, "What was it
like to have 'Free Will?'"

He says, "In the beginning, the
'Great I Am' was our first and only
thought. The gift of "Free Will" helped
us to avoid restrictions and limitations in
finding 'I am' within our inner being.
We were free to see 'I am', talk with 'I
am', share in what 'I am' knew, grow
together in harmony, and experience 'I
am's Love-light deeply within us."

I ask Eve, "Did you experience 'Free
Will this way?"

She says, "Yes, because of 'Free Will,'
the 'Great I Am' was our reality and our
awareness. At first I didn't see it as a
choice, but I suppose the choice was
always there, between the reality of 'I am's
presence and the illusion of something
more, something greater. Whatever that

something else was, it was only an unconscious mystery. Our life with 'I am' was wonderful. Our life was 'I am'. We had all we needed and wanted for nothing."

"How was the Dragon Lady able to tempt you then?" I ask.

Adam looks me in the eye, "She lied! The Dragon Lady makes me look at the mystery. She tells me there is much, much more than what we have in paradise. She tells me that we are much greater than we can imagine. In fact, she says that we are higher than the angels and the 'Great I Am' puts us over them. She says that we have a powerful knowledge that is even greater than the 'Great I Am's. She says that knowledge will help us to know the 'Great I Am' better than 'I am' knows Himself. She then offers to throw in a thing called 'ego' to help us see our superiority. She says that the ego will make us feel more confident. When I explained all this to Eve, I imagine what wonderful conversations we can have with the 'Great I Am.'

I ask, "Eve, when Adam tells you all this, what is your reaction?"

Eve responds quickly, "At first, I have

a gut feeling, an inner voice telling me, 'This is not a good thing.' But, the more she tells me the more it begins to sound like a great adventure. And remember, at that time we don't know what a lie is. The Dragon Lady convinces us it is the right thing to do. So, we buy into the deal and everything changes. Now, I can say it was not for the better."

Adam jumps in, "That 'great knowledge' turns out to be our rational thoughts, which is constantly dominating us and thinks it knows everything."

Eve adds, "And the chattering of the ego turns out to be a controlling little voice that won't give us a moment's peace. It has us off center constantly."

Adam continues, "In the blink of an eye, our realities reverse. Our rational thoughts and ego emerge from the shadows and declare themselves as our conscious reality, and our connection with the 'Great I Am' within us becomes a myth. The rational thoughts and ego blocks us from seeing 'I am' or talking with 'I am'."

Eve interjects, "'I am's presence seems to be gone. And suddenly we are out in the cold. Our paradise disappears. We must search for our food, find shelter, and make our clothes. We have to learn to do for ourselves."

Adam says, "I go off in search of the 'Great I Am' not knowing where to look. 'I am' disappears, and I can't find 'I am' anywhere. I call out 'Great I am' from the top of every mountain, but 'I am' does not answer. All I hear is the echo of my own voice. Then, my rational thoughts make me begin to wonder if it was all an illusion."

Eve says, "Adam is gone for days and comes home with little or nothing. It is real, all right, I can feel the chill right down to my bones. And this ego voice keeps saying that we didn't need 'I am' anyway. The ego makes it all about our right to control freedom of will and have what we want, when we want it. The truth is, we now long for what we need, because we didn't even have that any longer."

Adam says, "We put ourselves first and allow the 'Great I Am' to drift into the background. What we don't realize is that we are binding ourselves to wanting and craving and in reality, are left with no Free Will at all. The 'Free Will' we had with 'I am' was gone forever and we didn't know how to go back."

Eve adds, "Slowly, I began to wonder why the plants, rocks and animals don't talk to me any longer."

Adam concludes, "It wasn't until we died that we discovered our mistake and made our connection again. I feel so sorry for all the humans who never make that connection and live a life in darkness."

Eve concludes, "We hope your meditation process will help many find the Love-light within them and reverse this negative spiral we started."

We embrace and they fade back into the 'Great I Am.'

The irony of this story is that the 'Great I Am' never left, but they are blind to 'I am's presence. Their rational thoughts and ego make it appear that 'I am' left. Those same rational thoughts and ego are blinding you today. Those same rational thoughts and ego are creating an endless string of gods, religions, rules, laws and false truths. Those same rational thoughts and ego are calling your myth a reality and your reality a myth.

In reality, the 'Great I Am' is within us, always has been and always will be. When we choose 'I am' every day, all our

Free Well requires is that we fallow 'I am's purpose (not a law, but the act of remaining steadfast and faithful to your choice), which is to follow 'I am'. Thus, begins the history of our Spiritual Journey to rediscover the 'Great I Am' within us.

CHAPTER 3
The Dark-side

I sit in silence meditating for a long time. I can still feel the presence of the 'Great I Am'. Only now there is a heaviness. 'I am' seems to be pondering something unlikeable in many humans.

Reflecting, 'I am' starts to speak to me again, "After Cain and Abel, I start to sense something dark developing in the human rational thoughts. There are dark thoughts and emotions. I use the word dark only because dark thoughts and emotions are not part of My Light, or part of my creation images.

"In creation darkness or blackness is the absence of light and the blackness in empty space is very peaceful, calming and inwardly warming. That is why blackness helps to produce sleep. However, the darkness in the human rational thoughts is something else. It is a product of the undirected rational thoughts and ego in humans.

"The human brain chatter, brain clutter, brain chaos and brain deception are a minor handicap compared to what is hiding underneath. There is something much darker in the human rational thoughts, which has slowly become the norm. Thus making any experience of the Love-light, they knew in Eden, a distant choice.

"There is a total disregard for the natural order of the planet and universe. There is an uncontrolled subconscious desire to destroy it or bend it to their abusive purposes.

"There is a willful ignorance of My presence and what is good, right and caring. They are prepared to worship anything and any god that suits their purposes.

"In the human rational thoughts, there are two dark enemies to the survival of the planet. One is greed, and the other is complacency. Greed will do anything to increase its wealth, abundance, extravagance, property, appetite and control of other humans and creatures. While, human complacency will do nothing to stop greed's destruction of the planet.

"The Dark-side of the human rational thoughts is a convenient vile for hatred's poison. Hatred can be set aside temporarily, but it is always there to flash up again. When humans allow hatred to fester in their rational thoughts and feed their anger with wrath and rage, they end up poisoning their own heart. This hatred is fatal and will destroy any possibility of connecting with Me within you.

"It can also be passed down from one generation to the next generation. In that way, the rational thoughts not only destroy the organism in which it lives; it uses that destruction to poison the rational thoughts of others.

"In a dark corner of their rational thoughts there lurks a craving for senseless violence toward humanity and creation. This produces an endless number of wars, killing for the sake of killing of both humans and animals, and the needless destruction of nature because it is in the way.

"The darkness contains a corrupted envy of whatever the other person has, thus producing an unquenchable thirst which destroys any possibility of satisfaction and a sense of fulfillment.

"There is a lust for sex without love and a lust for power and domination. These lusts, humanity turns into religions.

"In the darkest corners of the human rational thoughts, there is their ability to rationalize and justify any human behavior."

I interrupt; knowing that 'I am' appreciates my interaction, "Are you describing what scholars call evil?"

I hear 'I am's addable hummm. Then 'I am' says, "I suppose I am avoiding that word. It is not in Me, or anything We created in the beginning. Basically, religious scholars and everyone else have so overused and misused the word evil that it has little or no meaning any longer. I could go on and on, like Eckhart Tolle, listing all the things it is not for a hundred pages and still not exhaust the subject."

I sense 'I am' already knows my next question, "Did the Dragon Lady cause this or know that it would happen?"

The tone in the 'Great I Am's voice becomes more loving when talking about her. "She definitely did not cause it to happen, but I am not sure if she was aware of the Dark-side before approaching Adam and Eve. One thing I am certain of is that she and her little devs, (The personification of the negative thoughts that can take over your rational thought.), quickly become masters at manipulating that side of the human rational thoughts.

"The devs are not a real entity. They are simply rational thoughts that are trying to take over the human body and mind. Through meditation, the body can shut them down."

"Do I understand you correctly that these dark thoughts do not exist in any other part of creation?" I ask the question, but it hits me immediately. I add, "Of course not. The thoughts of all animals, creatures, plants and rocks are tied completely to the Natural Order. Ego and hatred simply don't exist in them."

The 'Great I Am' confirms it, "Right, it is totally a product of the human rational thoughts and ego. I would also add; it is the opposite of everything I know about the Divine Mother."

"O.K. you said that the Dragon Lady gave Adam and Eve their rational thoughts and ego, and the rational thought in humans created their Dark-side. Then what role does she have in the process? I am constantly fighting off her presence."

"She is manipulating the human rational thoughts and ego by pushing them toward the Dark-side. She or her little devs become part of the brain chatter. I sense that she is only setting their rational thought and ego in motion. Once started they take on a life of their own. But you must remember that they are the myth, and everything else is the reality. The body can shut them down in meditation.

"When you meditate the body, its breathing, its presence, its awareness can shut down the chatter of the rational thoughts and ego and create stillness. Without stillness, humans cannot hear My voice and therefore lose any awareness of My presence. In fact, the human rational thoughts live in denial that awareness is one of the senses, while in the rest of creation it is the most important sense.

"When she discovers she can manipulate the human rational thoughts; she starts driving them to their extreme. With her help, the human rational thoughts and ego declare their thoughts as all-powerful. They can do anything. They can understand everything. They are the only reality. Their human thoughts are the proof of their own existence. Therefore, everything else is a myth. Note that that is a rational thought, a deductive logical thought that proves nothing.

"Look at the things her manipulation produces: the worship of sex; endless wars over nothing; the justification of slavery; the acceptance of ruling classes; the destruction of entire species; the destruction, pollution and poisoning of nature; the creation of countless false gods; the never ending theological creation of religions based on myths instead of a real connection to Me."

"If this is not evil, what do we call it?"

The 'Great I Am' starts to laugh, "I am inclined to call it the human Darkside."

I quickly respond, "But that only describes where it is, not what it is, the actions it produces or how it occurs."

I sense 'I am's enjoyment of the exchange, "Very good point, which reminds Me of a moment long ago. All of creation has already named it, evil. It wasn't long after Adam and Eve left Eden, until all the animals and creatures, both domestic and wild, came to Me to ask, 'What are you going to do about the evil of humans?' The plants came to ask, 'How long must we endure the senseless destruction of the human evil?' Even the stones came asking, 'Why are evil humans using us to kill each other?' So how can we define the word evil which is not part of Me or creation?"

Let me try, "Evil exists only in the Dark-side of the human rational thoughts and is produced by their rational thoughts and ego."

"That's a good start," 'I am' says.

"Evil actions emerging from the Dark-side of the human rational thoughts include: murder, hatred, wrath, power mongering, lust, abuse, greed, lying, stealing, slandering, gossiping, envy, delusion, egotism, to cling to false doctrine, material attachment, to work against or avoid a connection with the 'Great I Am'."

'I am' responds, "That's the best list I have ever heard, but I would change 'lust' to 'sexual lust', because a person can have a lust for life with Me."

"Good 'sexual lust' it is," I agree. "Evil occurs when a person willfully turns to the Dark side of the human rational thoughts."

'I am' suggests, "I like that, but add 'However, this can be reversed.' People can choose the way out of their Dark-side."

"The Positive-side and the Dark-side of the human rational thoughts must always co-exist. Therefore, evil is a human choice. The opposite choice is always open and possible. Consequently, there is no such thing as an evil person."

Now 'I am' is sending me positive energy. 'I am' responds, "perfect!"

I add, "The war between good and evil, or the Positive-side vs. the Dark-side of the human rational thoughts, is a constant in human life. Every human must constantly make that choice."

'I am' reacts, "I like this."

I say confidently, "The war between good and evil, as a cosmic conflict between two entities, is a myth created by human rational thoughts and the ego. The purpose of this myth is to mask the existence of the Dark-side of the human rational thoughts."

'I am' says, "Let Me consider the word 'mask', maybe 'hide' is better?" 'I am' pauses for a moment, "No 'mask' is a better image word." 'I am' adds, "Don't forget. 'Evil does not exist anywhere else in creation.' This is great."

'I am' is glowing inside me now.

'I am' adds, "It creates a clear picture of what evil is in all its forms and who is responsible."

I shut my ego down and ask, "So what did you decide to do about her manipulation of the Dark-side?"

"Over the ages, I struggle to reestablish My connection, but humans become more primitive and further and further away from what they knew in Eden. They lose all awareness of My presence. They lose their ability to speak the languages of the animals, creatures, plants, stones and soil. They suppress most of their natural instincts.

"I wait and wait and wait inside every human hoping to be discovered. Meanwhile, I enjoy all of nature and their connection with Me. I nudge and push humans when I can. I watch humans discover bronze and iron. Mostly on their own, they finally learn to write. These last two sentences describe the total accomplishments of the human race after receiving the Dragon Lady's higher knowledge. Their perceived knowledge makes the Dragon Lady's Big Lie laughable, but no one is laughing, millennium after millennium." 'I am' becomes silent.

I wait patiently and continue to listen. 'I am's light within me starts as a

glowing red color. Then it becomes a
bright yellow. I wait and listen. Finally,
'I am's light becomes a bedazzling white
and encompasses me.

'I am' concludes, "We have a lot of
work to do to untie this knot. Hopefully,
this Meditation Bible will help."

CHAPTER 4
The Roadblocks Part 1

Free Will vs. Freedom of Will

Now, 'I am' wants me to address the greatest roadblocks that we all face in reaching our 'Great I Am' center. These roadblocks are the deliberate creation of our rational thoughts and ego.

The first roadblock is our perception of what choice we have and how should we make it. There is great confusion as to the difference between "Free Will" and our rational choice of "freedom of will." You need to see how they emerged in order to get past them.

The second roadblock is our "Controlling Rational thoughts." This is the source of our "freedom of will," but how did we get it and could it be binding us with false perceptions?

The third roadblock is the "Controlling Ego." Where does it come from and what is it doing? How and why is it controlling us?

I will show you how to get past these roadblocks. But first, we need to be aware of what we are up against and what we must do to get past the roadblocks. The solution demands radical action and total commitment.

In the story of creation, the 'Great I Am' tells us what happened. We see the Mind of the 'Great I Am', which contains the Light and an image of all things in creation. These images are **not** rational thoughts. They are detailed blueprints beyond our human comprehension. We see the Love and life blood of the Divine Mother, which activates the Light and produces the Wording Son, who words all things into being from the inside out. All three are one and necessary for creation to take place. From all three, the reality of all things is formed. Light, Love, Life and existence happens.

Then the Divine Mother thrusts a thorn of hatred into the unity and the oneness. She becomes the Dragon Lady. She reveals rational thought to Adam and Eve and then throws in the free gift of the ego. Through our rational thoughts and ego, we think we are able to control all humanity and dominate the planet from the dark side of our rational thoughts. To maintain control over us, her gift of rational thought and an ego is manipulating humanity by encouraging us to create these roadblocks.

All the rest of creation is free of this rational thought and ego gift. They are in harmony with the natural order. While we, humanity, willfully and ignorantly destroy the planet all by ourselves. How can we stop this?

Let us unravel these roadblocks, that have been in the making since the beginning of time: the confusion between "Free Will" and "freedom of will;" the false perception that our rational thought is superior to all else; and the manipulation of the self by the controlling ego.

Free Will

"Free Will" is our choice to accept a connection with the 'Great I am' within us and fulfill the purpose that 'I am' has for us, or to go our own way.

In the beginning, the 'Great I Am' was our first and only thought. The gift of "Free Will" helped us to avoid restrictions and limitations in finding 'I am' within our inner being. We were free to see 'I am', talk with 'I am', share in what 'I am' knew, grow together in harmony with 'I am' and all of nature, and experience 'I am's wonderful Love-light. This was our reality. Our presence with 'I am' in the world was our reality. Our relationship with all things and care of them was our reality. We spoke the languages of all creatures, plants, rocks and soil. We knew them as well as they knew us.

The choice was always there to live in the reality of 'I am's presence or go our own way. Yes, the 'Great I Am' was our reality and part of our awareness. Our rational thoughts and ego were only a mental delusion or mystery.

Experience the creation story this way, and it will start to take on a new dimension. To this day our "Free Will" has not changed. It is still there. It is still the real reality. It is still ours, if we can find it.

Freedom of Will

Note that the Biblical metaphor of the tree of "Knowledge of Good and Evil," is in itself a rational choice. Rational choice gives us the mental allusion of our right to eat or not to eat the fruit. To choose evil over good. What Adam and Eve couldn't see in reality is that they were choosing between "Free Will" and the myth of "freedom of will." When Adam and Eve made that choice, our reality changed.

We reversed our perception of reality. Our rational thought emerged from the shadows and declared itself as our mental reality, and our Devine connection became our mythical imagination. With our rational thought, we made it all about our right to control "Free Will" by replacing it with our "freedom of will" to do whatever we please. We put ourselves first and allowed the 'Great I Am' to drift into the background. With your rational thoughts, we can create both sides of the rational choice. Throughout history, this allowed us to create an unending list of gods, an endless list of laws and an endless number of religions.

As time passes we form religious institutions to compartmentalize and control our perception and experience of God (no longer the 'Great I Am'). The leaders forming the institutions take the simple presence of 'I Am' and convert it into doctrine and dogma. All doctrine and dogma are of human creation and designed to control the beliefs of others, their understanding, and their experience of God. We use our "freedom of will" to bind ourselves in spiritual chains and create a great chasm between us and the

'Great I Am' within us. We create an all-powerful sky God, a mythical God of our own rational imagination. Our rational choice elevates its self as divine law, obeying, or not obeying a "Do Not" command.

For example, the 'Great I Am' wrote, for Moses, ten positive words on two tablets. Ten words to live by. Yet the religious leaders using "freedom of will" turn eight of them into "Don't do this and that." They take the one word for "Honor Life" and change it to "Do not kill," and then because they wanted to hate and kill in war, they changed it again to "Do not murder."

Summery of "freedom of will" and "Free Will"

In the Apostle John's word, we "sin." (The word sin, αμαρτανε /amartane, is a Greek archer's term meaning to miss the mark.) We miss the mark, the spiritual bull's-eye. Instead of seeking a relationship with the 'Great I Am' within us, seeing 'I am', talking with 'I am', walking with 'I am', loving 'I am', and being loved by 'I am', we choose our rational thoughts and ego. We choose a

God of our own creation and will do it endlessly.

Ironically, any knowledge of Good and Evil, white and black, becomes lost in a sea of gray. We are turning our backs on the 'Great I Am' just as the religious leaders turned their backs on Joshua. We have been turning our backs on 'I am' ever since. (This distinction is an underlying theme in the Gospel of John, and in particular chapters 6.)

Our "freedom of will" is not "Free Will." Our rational choice is only a leaning in one direction or another on a white to black line. A person may say, "I accept Jesus as my personal savior. I am born-again." But they don't change anything in their lives. They still have all the same hatreds, the same prejudices, and the same false perceptions that they have always had.

Many will even justify these actions as being done in the name of Joshua or God. Peter literally curses such people (2 Peter 2:20-21). They don't even realize that there is no hatred in the 'Great I Am'. There is no prejudice in the 'Great I Am'. There is no self-service in the 'Great I Am'.

Why is this true? The hatred is all

ours and part of our "dark side." As humans, we have a monopoly on prejudice. It exists only in us and is part of our "dark side." The bottom line is, we want to **think** we have "freedom of will" to choose between love or hate, equality or prejudice, being selfless or self-serving, when in reality, they are all part of the same behavioral line with light and dark ends. All we are doing is suppressing one and focusing on the other. That has nothing to do with "Free Will."

As a human race, we gave up on "Free Will" a long time ago. Adam and Eve turned their backs on the 'Great I Am' and walked away. And ever since, we have been doing the same thing over and over again. And that includes all religious institution and their leaders. For example, the modern Christian leaders and believers are no different than the Chief Priest, Scribes and Pharisees of 2000 years ago.

CHAPTER 5
The Roadblocks Part 2

<u>Rational thoughts</u>
<u>(Knowledge/Wisdom)</u>

The expansion of our knowledge doesn't help us. We now think of our knowledge and rational thoughts as all powerful. We can perceive anything, create anything, and do anything. In today's world, many have the false perception that our rational thought is superior to all else. Many Hindu and Buddhist sects have made this their highest goal, with ultimate knowledge equaling enlightenment.

In the middle ages, religious institutions pit themselves against the scientific community, while both are doing the same thing, pushing their mental/intellectual agendas. Ironically, the scientific community didn't realize that they were using inductive logic and not deductive logic. Which puts them outside any rational thought and "freedom of will."

Religious institutions conceived elaborate theologies based only on their human perception of a mythical being, whom they call God. He was a God somewhere up there, out there, beyond us, and all powerful, all knowing, a superior extension of our own rational thoughts. All those who would not embrace these theologies and dogmas were condemned and cast out of "the church." Today we can form new religions without an end in sight all over nothing and do the same thing all over again. The classic example is in Gulliver's Travels by Jonathan Swift, where the Big-endian and the Little-endian created a new church over their dispute as to witch end of the egg should be cracked. As funny as it may seem, I have actually seen it happen.

Likewise, the scientific community made substantial breakthroughs in the knowledge of our planet and the universe. It didn't matter that many of these were accidental. Unfortunately, the rational thoughts and egos of the scientists were eager to take all the credit. And like their theological counterparts, they were happy to blow a scientific theory into a law. It didn't matter that one theory gave way to a new theory in just a few years. A new law was raised in the name of scientific progress. Today we have a science of just about everything. To mention just a few of the most bizarre: Political Science, Behavioral Science, Science of Sleep, Science Olympiad, Science of Daydreaming, Science of Nose-picking, etc., etc....

There is no end to what our rational thoughts can do. We can create a computer and program it with all our knowledge and then call the computer all-knowing or super intelligent. But it is nothing more than a dumb device that can't even think. Even though there are many that think it thinks.

Fortunately, today many of the sciences are now focusing solely on their inductive observations and making major breakthroughs. They set their labs and research up to show the actual results, which take science to the next level. They are no longer trying to prove a point to justify a preconceived notion.

Rational thought has created its own sciences, like psychology, philosophy and Education, which are not sciences at all. They are only seeking to perfect rational thought and produce ultimate Wisdom.

That's it! If you have ultimate Wisdom, you will have ultimate power. As Nietzsche said, "If you have Wisdom

you are Superman, you are God." Our
all-powerful knowledge is leading us to
Wisdom, and there lies the rub.

Throughout history the 'Great I Am'
has repeatedly broken through this
"rational choice" myth. 'I am' has made
it clear that real knowledge is within the
'Great I Am' center of all things,
including humans. When we connect to
the 'Great I Am' within us, and only then,
we become part of the full knowledge of
the creator.

In 1 Thessalonians 2:13, Paul uses
Isiah's image, "You took the 'I Am's'
words into your heart. You realized that
the 'I Am' is at work within you."

Joshua is telling us, "Wisdom belongs
to the Father, the 'I Am' within you. 'I
am' is your teacher. Only through 'I am'
do you receive true knowledge."

Throughout history there are a few
who see this basic truth.

Plato tells this story about his teacher
Socrates in *The Apology*. He wrote it
about 500 years before Joshua's birth. Yet
it speaks to the question of rational
thought and wisdom as raised here and in
the scriptures. The conclusion is
identical. Plato writes,

Socrates heard that the Oracle at Delphi said, "Socrates is the wisest of men."

Socrates considered this a slander against him and went to call on the Oracle at Delphi in order to set the record straight. He asked the Oracle, "Surely someone is wiser than I?"

The Oracle replied, "No one is wiser."

Socrates reflected, "What does the Oracle mean by this? This riddle doesn't make sense. I know that I am not wise at all. So, what could the Oracle mean by saying I am the wisest? Surely an Oracle would not lie. That is forbidden."

Socrates puzzled over the meaning for a long time. Finally, with great reluctance, he decided to look into the matter and put it to the following test.

He went to a person renowned for his wisdom, a certain unnamed politician. He thought, "Surely this man is wiser, and I can tell the Oracle that she is mistaken that I am the wisest."

Socrates examined this politician. He seemed to be wise to many who gathered around him. And he considered himself especially wise. Unfortunately, he was not. When he tried to show him the error of his thinking, the politician

72

hated him for it, along with many
of his protégés.

Socrates left thinking, "I am wiser
than that man. Yet neither of us
knows anything useful. While he
thinks he knows something and
actually does not, I know I don't
know anything and do not think I
do. Therefore, it would appear
that I am wiser on this minor
point; I do not think I know what I
do not."

Socrates continued his test and
examined a renowned scholar.
Many considered the scholar even
wiser than the politician was. To
his surprise, he found the scholar
to be exactly the same. He
thought he knew when in reality
he did not. He also considered
himself especially wise. Again,
when he pointed out the error in
his logic, the scholar and his many
protégés hated him.

Socrates recalls, "I pressed on,
even though I knew, regretted, and
feared that people hated me. I
had to put the Oracle to the test,
thus, searching out all those with
a reputation for knowledge. What
I discovered was that those
considered most renowned for
their wisdom, turned out to be the
most deficient. While those
reputedly inferior showed
themselves to be more

knowledgeable."

In his continued wandering, Socrates tested the great poets, accomplished in all their art forms. He thought, "Surly I will discover myself to be less wise by comparison. So, I studied poems in which I thought they had revealed some profound content. I asked them what they meant, so I could learn from them. Unfortunately, anyone present could have given me a better explanation than the poets produced. That is how I came to realize that poets do not make poems by wisdom, but rather by some emotional feeling or divine inspiration, exactly like visionaries and prophets. While the latter may reveal many fine things, they don't claim to know anything of what they speak. However, the poets turned out to be quite different, because of their poetry they considered themselves the wisest of men in other matters, and were not. Once again, I appeared wiser on this minor point, the same as with the politician."

Socrates' final test was with the craftsmen. He said, "I was aware that my knowledge in these areas was little or nothing, but I was certain that they knew many things

*and had fine skills. They rose to
my expectations, with knowledge
of many things beyond my
experience, and in that regard,
were wiser than I am. However,
they had the same failing as the
poets. While they practiced their
own crafts well, they each
considered themselves wise in
other things, things of significant
importance. This mistake
diminished their wisdom.*

*"Thus, out of fairness to the
Oracle, I asked myself whether I
could accept myself for who I am,
being neither wise with their
wisdom nor foolish with their
folly. Or, whether I could accept
wisdom and folly together, and
become like them. I answered,
both for myself and the Oracle, 'It
was better to be as I am.'"*

The hatred grew against Socrates
and the slander continued that he
was wise. Whenever he tested
others, those people present
assumed that he was wise in those
things. Socrates proclaimed, "In
reality, it is only the Oracle who is
wise. By her oracle she is saying,
'Human nature is worth very little
or nothing at all.' It is obvious
that she does not mean this fellow
Socrates is wisest. She only uses
my name as an example. What
she is really saying is, 'Anyone

among you is wise, who knows as Socrates knows that his wisdom is nothing.'

"To this day, I go about testing others on behalf of the Oracle, searching, and questioning both citizens and strangers. When I find someone who is wise, or one who is not, I help the Oracle to prove it. Because of this endeavor, I have no leisure time for the affairs of state or my own financial gain. Thus, I live in utter poverty because of my service to the Great I Am."

(STORIES OF YOUR SPIRIT, VOL I; Revitalizing Ministries, NH; pp. 277ff)

We can all consider ourselves tested. If I had to give a penny away for every scholar, religious or pious person that I have met who claimed to be wise, I would be as poor as Socrates was. Only the 'Great I Am' is wi...

Oops, 'I am' interrupts, "No, I am not! I have no need of rational thought. It is useless."

You see, we have much to learn as 'I am's students.

Many quote Plato throughout history, "He is wise who knows as

Socrates knows that his wisdom is nothing."

Could it be that all our pursuits of rational knowledge are a pursuit of nothingness?

O yes, now I hear 'I am' laughing.

CHAPTER 6
The Roadblocks Part 3

Controlling Ego

Now let's take a look at our controlling ego. As a free bonus, the Dragon Lady threw into the bargain the ego, and we accepted it. What we didn't realize was that we were **binding** ourselves to a wanting and craving of everything. And, I do mean everything there is, from having what you need to having great wealth, from having a good meal to stuffing your face, from importance and leadership to absolute power, from doing your best to winning without scruples, from looking for abiding Love to seeking quick sexual satisfaction, etc. etc. etc.

While in the pseudo ego reality of our rational thoughts, we try to cut ourselves off from our harmony with everything else on the planet. We want what we want and we want it now. We want it all.

There are many parts to the ego. Our ego is perhaps the most difficult part of the roadblock.

Set aside the Psychological treatise on ego by Jung and Freud. They are both false perceptions of rational thought.

The ego is the rational brain-chatter coming from our dark side.

The ego is not an entity. It is simply part of rational thought on the left side of the brain. It will not tolerate any entity as greater than itself.

In the case of Nietzsche, his ego convinced him that God is dead. This created a tsunami that raced through the theological community. However, as I finished my study of his works, the 'Great I Am' within me was laughing. 'I am' said, "You do realize that Nietzsche is dead. I look in on him every day."

The ego in all of us is exactly the same in each of us. It is saying to us, "The Great I Am within you!? Well maybe, 'as you.'" Or it says, "Are you Mental? YOU are the most important person on this planet, the most important thing."

I don't care who you are, high or low in social standing, rich or poor, strong or weak, more or less intelligent, at some point you bought into this ego rhetoric. And once convinced, it is very difficult to set aside.

The ego always WANTS more. The body may need food, water, and shelter, but the ego wants more and better food, cleaner water, and a more lavish dwelling. Your ego says, "I want you to be happy. I want you to have that BMW." So you get the BMW. But the ego is not satisfied with having. It only wants more. After a month or two, It says to you, "It's only a BMW, you deserve better." It has been said, "Too many people spend money they don't have on buying things they don't need to impress people they don't like." The problem with this part of the ego is that most people are not even aware of its influence. To put it in perspective, imagine how many people bought a lottery ticket in the last ten minutes.

The ego must feel superior. Every action the ego has you take is designed to create a feeling of superiority. To the ego, equality is not enough. You are number one, the ONE. The obvious examples are: winning at all cost, taking drugs if necessary; doing anything to get that promotion or pass that test, lying and cheating if you have to; destroying others to get to the top, passing the blame when necessary; and throwing ethics to the wind to produce a higher bottom line, calling embezzlement "creative bookkeeping."

The subtle actions and the most damaging are the ones that spill out without a thought, like name calling, "stupid," "punk," "bastard," "bitch," "jerk." The list is endless. Gossiping is one of the worst. All it does is stroke the ego of the teller. The same is true of a put-down-comment and sarcasm, the lowest form of humor, unless you can make the sarcasm about yourself.

The ego will have you think, it is never wrong. With an active ego, the less information a person has the more it talks and won't let the other person get a word in edgewise. The ego would rather invent facts and statistics than appear wrong. Distorting facts and misdirecting attention is another tactic of a want-to-be-right ego.

The ego can justify anything. In our modern society this has reached horrific levels and global proportions. We can rationalize and justify absolutely anything from: mass genocide, to raping, and abusing children, to abusing women.

The ego will go to any lengths to protect itself. Here are just a few of the identifiers: "I must protect my way of life;" "It's in the National interest;" "The Bible says...;" "Everyone is doing it;" "I did nothing wrong;" and "It is within the law." This has become so easy for most people that they are now borderline sociopaths.

To be self-serving is a product of the ego, and we are the only entity on the planet that has one. Our ego is a major part of our "dark side." It is very easy to lean toward "Me, Myself, and I," and that is what most people do without giving it a second thought. What is the first thing that your ego thinks of when you are about to come into a large sum of money? "What can I buy for myself?" I have seen many self-serving egos spend all the money before the deal is closed. When they never get the money, it makes their slide to the "dark side" even darker.

All these parts of the ego are there to do one thing, control us. I warn you, the ego will not give up control without a fight. To understand what you are up against, remember the ego is the free gift we got from the Dragon Lady. To make it even more difficult, when your rational thoughts and ego combine forces they are almost unstoppable.

But it can be done! Be aware!

Yes, you know a lot of people who fit these descriptions, and at first it may seem funny as you think of them. But, do they describe you in any way. Too often we become blind to the flaws in our selves. That is a problem.

It is possible for a person to be aware of what the ego is doing in any of these situations. But how? We need to become the observer, see it and then shut it down. We need to step out of our rational thoughts and experience things within our body, our own behavior, as the observer. We need to find the silence within our body, the dark vastness of space within our center, the warm pool of nothingness, the tiny speck of Love-light that is the 'Great I Am', not the SELF. Find those things and shut the ego down. That doesn't mean that it is easy to stop the ego. Once it gets on a roll, we need to double our awareness.

Some will say, "the ego can't be all bad. I can use my ego to do good things. I can use it to give more, lead better, have great wisdom and fill myself with more love."

No matter how much a person rationalizes the actions of their ego, their ego is always a liar and deceiver. Sacred literature is loaded with examples. The wealthy man who gave more than the

poor widow who gave only three pennies.
The King who declared himself God and
demanded his subjects worship him.
And, the wise King Solomon who had
1000 wives and never knew love, but he
lived a life full of sexual passion. The very
act of raising the ego as a good thing is in
its self an act of egotism.

CHAPTER 7
The Solution, Part 1

To tackle these roadblocks, I recommend that you do so in the reverse order. See yourself as untying a knot that has been many millennia in the tying. This knot cannot be untied with a sword. There are three steps in this process: neutralizing the ego; controlling your rational thought; and rediscovering your true "Free Will" connection with the 'Great I Am' again.

Neutralizing the Ego

Challenging your ego is perhaps the most difficult thing you will ever do. It can't be tamed. It can't be destroyed until the day you die. But, it can be neutralized by observing it in action. That means you must work constantly to keep it neutralized. It is perfectly capable of rearing its influence without warning and reasserting its control over you in a nanosecond.

Your greatest tool for neutralizing your ego is your <u>natural</u> body. (The term natural here means free of drugs and other debilitating or addictive substances. It is the form in which you were created.)

Health, fitness, and a good diet are strong allies to the body. In fact, you will discover that your body is already screaming at you for help to correct problems – illness, lack of exercise and a poor diet. Your body wants you to be healthy, fit, and eat the right things.

Unlike your ego, your body will never lie to you. While there are a few body functions that use the brain, like our senses, most of the body functions work on their own, with the brain only acting as an observer in some cases, like the heart beating, breathing, blinking, reflexes, hunger, thirst and tiredness.

In fact, your body is talking to you all the time, and most people are unaware or prefer to ignore it. The nineteenth century theory that the body is your "animalistic" nature, is completely false and a fabrication of your rational thoughts and ego.

Below, you will have the opportunity to learn how to listen to your body and shut down those rational thoughts and ego.

In addition to learning how to listen to your body, you also need to rediscover your natural breathing to shut down your ego. Your ego is constantly misdirecting you when it comes to your breathing. For example, your coach, leader, or doctor asks you to take a deep breath, and you puff up your chest and suck in a little bit of air. Your ego thinks you look great when you are doing this. But, in reality you are not taking a deep breath at all. The ego is lying to you.

To take a deep breath, blow out all the air you can and relax. The body will take a deep breath all by itself.

This is how it works. Your body knows how to breath. You don't need to do anything. You cannot stop it, even if you wanted to. To experience this lay down on your back, place your hands on your upper abdomen just below the ribcage, and relax. Soon you will notice that your hands are moving up on the inhale and down on the exhale. To take a deep breath, push down with your hands and force all the air out of your body. Now just relax. Your body will take the deep breath all by itself. This the way your body breaths while you are sleeping.

If you try to hold your breath, you will ultimately gasp for air or pass out, and the body will take the breath for you. Experience what the body is doing, how it feels, and note that your rational thoughts and ego are not doing any of it.

In the second meditation tutorial, you will learn how to breath naturally. You will learn how to let you natural breathing take over, and it will shut down your rational thoughts and ego.

You may even experience a lightness of being. The whole world will change around you. Your ego will be neutralized. Your body will emerge confident and in charge of your physical being. It will become your greatest ally.

Others will see you differently and they will be drawn to you. Enjoy this feeling; enjoy the new connection with others; but avoid the mistake of using it to feed the ego. The moment your rational thoughts and ego say you're superior, more powerful than others, have more Facebook friends than others or more control over others, you will have made that mistake. Fortunately, the next steps will help you overcome or avoid any such problems.

Controlling our Rational Thought

The brain has many functions, and each function is predominantly in a specific part of the brain. Only the left part of the brain has the rational mind and scientific thought. Rational thought uses deductive logic, while scientific thought uses inductive logic, based on observation and mathematics.

Rational thought and ego are the only parts of the brain giving us any problems. As we saw earlier in creation, this was the gift of the Dragon Lady.

The irony is that rational thought likes to think that it is the only part of any significance in the brain. You can find a fitting example of this in the nineteenth century with the rise of "the age of reason." As Descartes famously put it "I think, therefore I am." Note the use of deductive logic here. He might as well say, "My ego told me, I exist."

Once you connect with your body, you can realize how laughable that hypothesis is. Rational thought can no more tell the heart to stop beating than it can tell the lungs to stop breathing.

Obviously, Descartes lacked the courage to doubt his rational thinking and philosophical wisdom. If he had, he might have understood Plato's quote of Socrates.

While many will falsely claim that rational thought has given us much in the past centuries, they fail to realize it has also blinded us as to whom we really are. It has filled us with hatred and violence, causing endless distrust, anger and war. Look closely at what it is telling you about your "enemy." Guess what? It is telling your enemy the exact same thing about you. We need to stop its constant chatter to unlock the true mysteries of our inner being.

Joshua and a few spiritual leaders, using the right brain, actually unlock these mysteries only to have the world turn their backs on them. That is how crippling the left brain rational thought can be.

In all recorded history, not one person's rational thought has come close to unlocking these mysteries. However, many scholars talk about some secret wisdom that holds the key. For most of those searching for that key, it is nothing more than a tilting with wind-mills.

However, the 'Great I Am' wants you to be aware that 'I am' is that key, and 'I am' is working in your right brain. Shut down the chattering rational thoughts and find 'I am' within you. Then connect and accept your life's purpose. That is the goal. Some have managed that with only a series of right choices. Others have found 'I am' totally by accident. A few struggle and suffer to achieve that end their whole lives and only get close.

At the same time, there have been countless individuals who have quieted their rational thoughts and achieved a great inner body awareness through meditation. At 'I am's suggestion, Meditation is the focus of this book.

Meditation is the major tool with which we can challenge and quiet our rational thoughts and ego. Traditionally, there are three things that many practices of meditation help you realize: learning to listen in silence and stillness; reduce the mind to one and only one pointedness; and move toward experiencing nirvana, a place of absolute nothingness. These three things can quiet the mind and bring you to that very special place within yourself.

This practice of meditation will take you one step further. It will help you find the Love-light in your inner being. This is the 'Great I Am' within you.

On my journey, the 'Great I Am' has me try many different meditation disciplines. They all work, with varying degrees of ease. Finally, 'I am' leads me to this practice that I share with you in this book.

This meditation eliminates the minds one pointedness. There are absolutely no thoughts. Your rational thoughts and ego are completely shut down. You are one hundred percent into your body and its breathing. That is where the 'Great I Am' is. Search and you shall find the Love-light.

In addition to the natural body care mentioned earlier, it is also important to supplement your meditation with some form of movement training, so the body stays fit and tuned into your meditation. This can be anything from yoga to one hour walks with your dog. It can be any physical training that works for you.

The **first** part of the solution is to learn to really listen to your body. Learn to listen to what it is telling you. Learn its language. This will give you a profound awareness of your inner being, and 'I am's presence within you.

The 'Great I Am' says, "I prefer that you call this awareness, because it precisely describes what you are doing, and what you gain from doing it. After all, it is your sixth sense. The terms 'consciousness' and 'enlightenment' are so misused they could lead you back into your rational thoughts and ego, which is the one thing you want to avoid."

Once you learn the body's language, it will tell you many things. It will show you what movements and body positions are in your genes. It will teach you what body positions are correct for your body. It will tell you when you slip into bad habits. It will help you shut down your rational thoughts and ego. Unlike them, it will never lie to you.

The **second** part of the solution is to focus your awareness on your natural breathing. Since your body breaths all by its self, it requires no thought. As mentioned above, you will be going one step beyond having one and only one thought. You will be having no thoughts at all.

Here is how it works. You become aware that your breath is going in and out, in and out, in and out. You are an observer on many levels. The body feels the air coming in and out. The ears hear the sound. The eyes see the movement. You are aware of the rhythm. You sense the energy pumping through your body.

All this you accomplish with the body alone. Not one rational thought contributes anything. Your rational thoughts may try to break in, but they are like a distant voice from another galaxy. You simply maintain your focus on what your body is saying and your natural breathing, and your rational thoughts and ego will fade out.

In a group meditation, after just a few minutes, you will be aware that everyone is breathing in exactly the same rhythm.

The **third** step will prepare you for finding the 'Great I Am.' Your breath is silently leading you to a Love-light within you. When you reach that Love-light, It will breathe new life into you and light up your life.

In the profound dialectic laid out in the collective works of Kierkegaard, you will find a description of what you will be going through. You will see that your rational thoughts and ego are your sickness unto death. You must pass through the fire. You will see the ironic error of it. You must pass through the fire. You will learn to laugh at it. You must pass through the fire. You will learn

to love it. You must pass through the fire.
Then you will destroy its hold over you, a
willful crucifixion of self, your rational
thoughts and ego, an acceptance of the
cross and turning yourself over to the
'Great I Am' within you. You will pass
through the fire and into the Love-light.
Only then will you discover the greatest
gift of Love you have ever known.

You will discover your 'Great I Am'
center. You will experience the 'Great I
Am' within you. You will realize that 'I
am's Presence and Heaven are within you.
'I am's Spirit will fill you with a Love-
light beyond all other experiences.

You will walk with 'I am'. You will
talk with 'I am'. As the Apostle
Bartholomew says, "Your rational
thoughts will explode into a million
pieces. Your heart will leap from your
breast into the hand of the 'Great I Am'.
You'll feel a Love so great you'll feel your
heart will burst. You'll experience a Light
so powerful that it will wash all the sins
from your soul." Every cell of your body,
every neuron of your brain will be forever
changed. The 'Great I Am' will introduce
you to your life's purpose and to the rest
of your life. Now the choice is yours, to
accept or decline 'I am's purpose for you.

As I make this discovery, my inner being realizes that Joshua' prayer (the Lord's Prayer) is only an outline, and this prayer floods out of me.

> Abba in my Inner Being,
> Let me embrace You this day,
> Let your Presence shine within me.
> Help me to share Your Love-light throughout the earth.
> Help me to gather the bread of life to feed everyone.
> Make forgiveness part of who I am.
> Help me bring Love-light to the Dragon Lady.
> Let Your Presence, Power, and Love-light endure forever.
> Yes! Yes! Yes!

Thus, begins every day, sitting in silence, emptying your rational thoughts and ego, and connecting with the Love-light within. It is not a onetime event. It is a new way of life. I now meditate several times an hour, sometimes for only ten seconds, other times for ten minutes. We walk together. We talk together. I fulfil my purpose.

Soon, you too will reach this point in your meditation. Now you have a CHOICE to make, and you will make it every day, every moment, for the rest of your life.

CHAPTER 8
The Solution, Part 2

Once you make your **connection** with the 'Great I Am' within you and **accept** 'I am's purpose for your life, everything is going to change. You will experience a Newness of Life. Slowly, you will need to let go of all your negative baggage, ideas and assumptions. Plus, you need to brace yourself for the most powerful Love relationship you will ever experience in this life time.

All day of every day, you will be making choices. Only now, those choices are your "Free Will" choices. Your "rational thought" choices, and your "freedom of will" choices are no longer acceptable. Let them go.

Free Will

"Free Will" is the choice which was given to us in creation.

Yes, the true "Free Will" was our original choice. It was our reality. Now, it can be your reality again. It is your right to choose to accept the purpose which the 'Great I Am' has for you, or blindly go your own path. During the everyday give and take with the 'Great I

Am' within you, you may choose to do it your way. That is real "Free Will." We all do it and learn from it.

I often wonder how 'I am' can be so patient with us, then 'I am' says, "Many times, I too am able to learn from you. That is the great strength of "Free Will," we learn from each other. Your life's purpose is a path we walk together. The most important thing we do is to listen to each other."

This is our new reality, which was our original reality. Does that mean that our rational thought and ego will go back to being the unconscious myth it was in creation?

No, but first, clearly see what your rational thoughts and ego do. Your rational thoughts and ego, will tell you that the 'Great I Am' is a figment of your imagination or a being outside yourself. To realize the irony of what your rational thoughts and ego are telling you, ask yourself these questions.

Have you ever seen someone's thoughts? Have you ever seen a thought of your own? Have you ever seen one of your ideas? Is it really like a light bulb? Yes, you have had a thought. Yes, you have had an idea. But they are only realized when you express them, and even then you only see them when you write them out or turn them into an object or something. Ironically, you still only see the product; you cannot see the thought or idea itself.

On the other hand, you just discovered the 'Great I Am' within you. That experience requires no external expression, because you physically see, feel and experience 'I am' within you. You may even want to shout it from the roof tops. So, which one is real?

Now, in this day and age, the presence and manipulation of our rational thoughts and ego is very real. It may not have substance, but its purpose is to take us over. And it has for many millennia. This makes the 'Great I Am' within you and your rational thoughts and ego both real. We cannot destroy our rational thought and ego. All we can do is shut them down or control them, rather than allow them to have control over us. Even then, they will rear their annoying influence whenever you let down your guard.

It is sad when we realize what Adam and Eve lost, and how easy they had it. But, we can have that again. All we need is 1% of the population to return to the 'Great I Am' and then the Devine Mother will return. With Her creation will continue. Only, we will be part of it.

For now, we can work with the 'Great I Am' to learn to use our other brain functions, especially our right brain, for 'I am's purposes. If we are open to this, 'I am' will help us push the human limits far beyond anything we can possibly imagine.

'I am' has already proven this throughout history, with many individuals. Most of these you will find in the new book, *FINDING THE LOVE-LIGHT* to be published soon.

Now, 'I am' is asking me to share one of these break-through-moments here. After Adam and Eve left the garden, the 'Great I Am' connected to Cain and Able. Then it took many millennia before anyone connected with 'I am'. This is how the first connection took place.

> 'I am' introduces those who connect, "Many millenniums pass, but finally, a middle-aged woman, with seven children, becomes aware of My Love-light within her. On her own, she learns how to shut down her rational brain chatter and ego. She then discovers an inner peace.

Her name is Devaki, and she is married to Vasudeva. He is not on the same path as Devaki, but he accepts and supports her. He can feel the profound changes occurring within her.

"One morning, before the rest of the family is awake, Devaki is moving deeper and deeper in her meditation. She moves past the moment of inner peace and finds herself bathing in, what she calls, 'the dark sea of nothingness'. She embraces the nothingness and soaks up the serenity.

"I appear as a speck of light floating through the vast nothingness. She sees Me and moves closer. She embraces the Light, and My Love-light quickly fills her entire body and mind. I call her by name, 'Devaki, can you hear Me?'

"She responds, 'Yes, Master. I am listening.'

"My joy explodes in a bedazzling Light, and I say, 'I am here within you. Connect with me and we can bring Light and Love back into the world.'

"She answers, 'Yes, Master...'

"At that moment an infant cries, and she quickly comes out of her meditation. She walks over and picks up a two-year-old baby. She comforts him. Just when I assume she broke the connection, she says,

'Master, this is my son Balarama.' I sigh, the connection is secure.

"I assure her, 'He shall always have my protection.'

"Without hesitation, she says, 'Thank you, Master.'

"My connection with her is a new beginning. Now, I start to put together a plan.

"For the next two days, our connection continues for most of the time. The Love-light grows within her, and she grows more and more positive, pushing back her Dark-side with Love. She tries to tell her husband about Me, but he finds it hard to believe. Fortunately, he encourages her to continue and promises to keep an open mind.

"On the third day, I have a plan. During the early morning, I appear to Devaki and Vasudeva in a dream. I explain that I will help them conceive their eighth son. He will be my first prophet, and they are to call him Krishna. He will bring the human race back to the Love-light and help people to connect with Me within them. He will neutralize the Dark-side in all humans. I let my Love overflow within both of them. They awaken and experience their most passionate lovemaking, and Krishna is conceived.

"From that moment on, Devaki bares in her womb her lotus-eyed son. All those who gaze upon her must turn their heads away from the blinding Light that fills her. Those who can stand to look on her radiance can feel the darkness in their rational thoughts turn and run away.

"Krishna is a pure delight from the day he is born in 3228 BCE. We connect, and he willingly fulfills My purpose for him. His Light is powerful, and he can drive off a dev creating a Dark-side in another human from a hundred paces. He nurtures the honor and equality of both men and women and insists on its acceptance. He becomes a living example of what it means to connect to Me, right up to his untimely death.

"My hopes are that his Love-light and life shall be an endless number of ripples on a quiet sea, which reaches and changes distant shores. Unfortunately, it is a small pebble thrown into an angry sea, which creates no ripples at all. At least that is the way it is until now."

This adds a new dimension to the original "Free Will" with 'I am' in your inner being. With 'I am', you can navigate the brain functions and use it to its fullest capacity, without the negative downside. The choice is yours and 'I am's together.

This dimension of "Free Will"

produces an interesting phenomenon. The 'Great I Am' always knows what you are thinking, planning, or doing, but 'I am' never knows what you're going to do, to 100%, until you do it. 'I am' can usually tell you the same thing about others weather they are connected or not, because 'I am' is present within everyone and everything. Obviously, this negates the myth that the God of rational thought is all knowing. In fact, it reveals that all the gods created by rational thought are basically mythical. However, for the most part, the founders of most religions were individuals connected to the 'Great I Am'.

You can choose to embrace the 'Great I Am' within you or turn your back. Marilyn Plowman expressed it succinctly in her poem "Free."

> We are free.
> Free
> Free
> Free
> FREE
> FREE
> F R E E!
> To be bound in whatever way we choose.

How are you bound? You may <u>think</u> your choice to connect, to fulfill the

'Great I Am's purpose for you, is only binding in the sense that any choice to do otherwise seems like an impossible possibility. That may have been the case in creation, but not now. Our rational thoughts and ego are existing ideas, chatter, dysfunctionality, or behavior we need to reckon with. You may get them under control, but you cannot destroy them.

Fortunately, the 'Great I Am' knows this and is all forgiving, with the Love-light always available to everyone. It doesn't matter if we go astray; we all do. 'I am' does not like it, if we turn or backs and walk away. 'I am' does not like it, if we go deep into our dark side. 'I am' is always there and always will be there for us and ready to welcome us back.

As George Lucas writes, even a character like 'Darth Vader' can walk away from the dark side and find the force, the Love-light again. There is no such thing as Divine wrath, punishment, or vengeance. There is no such thing as judgement day. To the 'Great I Am', our estrangement is punishment enough, since our estrangement is self-inflicted.

'I am' explains it to me this way, "When you die, there is no judgment; I

only ask one question, which is, 'Have you forgiven yourself for all your sins (every time you missed the mark)?'"
Wow, that sounds easy.

Sometime later, I missed the mark and found myself rationalizing my way around it until I convinced myself that I did nothing wrong. Then it hit me, oops, now I will forget that I ever did it and the mark will be there for all eternity. I quickly unraveled my rationalization, recognized my sin and forgave myself. It felt fantastic. The latter only took ten seconds. The rationalization was ten days in the making and felt terrible.

Then you ask, "What is Hell?"

Hell is going a lifetime without ever connecting to the 'Great I Am' within you and being trapped in your rational thoughts and ego. Then after death, you will spend all eternity in the darkness of the bottomless pit stuck in the tar of rational nothingness. Only now in the distance, you can see all those enjoying the Love-light and enjoying each other. But there is no way for you to get there. That is Hell.

How many times have you heard someone ask these questions? What is the meaning of life? Who am I? What is the purpose of my life? When we are young these seem like profound questions. Once you have met the 'Great I Am,' you realize that they are rational thought trivia. The story of the young Samuel says it all. The 'Great I Am' called out, "Samuel, Samuel!" Samuel responds instantly, "Yes? I'm here."

You are standing there with the 'Great I Am' inside you. You are one with 'I am'. 'I am' is one with you. 'I am' has always been there since the beginning of creation and always will be for all eternity.

When I first realized this, I blushed. 'I am' was right there for my first kiss to every big or small event in my life. It seems impossible that anyone could walk away from 'I am' in their inner being any more than a tree could. Yet you can, and you will; that's your "Free Will."

You will make this choice every day, every moment for the rest of your life. The big difference between you and Adam and Eve is that you now have the tools to find your way back. The chains on your false "freedom of will" are gone forever.

If you give yourself to the 'Great I Am' within you, that means you will let the 'Great I Am' give you your life's purpose. You will allow 'I am' to guide your life, with "Free Will" always there as a choice.

Try to envision a world in which the 'Great I Am' is driving the bus instead of our rational thoughts and egos. If we think we have come a long way in the past centuries, it will only be a grain of sand compared to what is to come. Perhaps at this moment the 'Great I Am' is giving that vision to one of you.

You won't always understand what you're being asked to do. Many times, your rational thoughts and ego will tell you it is ridicules or even insane. I recommend that you do them anyway. Always, I look back on those moments and find myself saying to the 'Great I Am', "So that's why you had me do that!" Not to mention the times I have had to say, "You were right. I should have listened."

Another thing which I find totally amazing, 'I am' will give me a project or a vision that I believed to be totally original, only to discover a year or so later that a world away someone else was given the same project or vision.

Specifically, one such thing happened

when I was given, while I was in Rode Island, the poem "In the Beginning" about the Devine Mother in creation. Two years later I was walking down the street in Annapolis, when I saw a painting in the window that told the same story. I walked in and asked to see the painting. Its title was "In the Beginning." I bought the painting and asked if I could contact the artist, Judy King Rieniets. I was told that they were expecting her any minute. She walked in the door. We met, talked a little, and she invited me for dinner.

I discovered that she too was connecting to the 'Great I Am' within her. She did the painting at the exact time I was writing the poem. She then told me the incredible story of how the painting just flowed out of her with her brush moving in a blur. The image was within her body. She said, "My hand and body were under Her control." She finished the painting in a little over an hour.

This is what the 'Great I Am' can do with you or anyone.

We are not isolated individuals in this process. You are going to realize that this is a universal possibility. At first it feels like a very personal experience to meet and connect with the 'Great I Am' within you. Then you realize, the 'Great I Am' is in everyone and everything. Oddly enough, every plant, creature, and object on the planet already knows this and lives by this. The human race is the only species still struggling to accept this simple truth; the 'Great I Am' is within us.

It is only natural that you will want to connect and share your experience with others who have connected with the 'Great I Am.' However, resist the temptation to rush off and start another religion. The world has had quite enough of that.

Each of our experiences is totally different and the 'Great I Am's purpose for each of us is different. Yet there is only one 'Great I Am' and we are all united in the 'I am'.

I find that those who are the most radically different from my experience are those who are the most interesting and exciting, because they make me realize how really Great the 'Great I Am' is.

At some point, you will realize that unity is the main purpose of the 'Great I Am,' unity with each other, unity with 'I am' and unity with everything on the planet. When that happens, your life will change forever.

Suddenly, you will be part of the bigger picture, the greater plan. Your name will be written in the great book of life. You will become one with 'I am's will, and 'I am' will say, "Welcome to the beginning of your Spiritual journey."

CHAPTER 9
The Meditation Process

The goal of this meditation process is to center yourself and find the 'Great I Am' within you. Once you find 'I am', you have the big Free Will choice to make, to accept 'I am's purpose for your life, or remain bound to your rational thoughts and ego. That is true Free Will.

Choose the 'Great I Am' and it will be like a second birth. You will be leaving behind all your old hatreds, false emotions, prejudices and misperceptions. You will be truly living in the Now. You will be living in the Love-light. Once you connect to 'I am', you will be making that choice every minute of every day for the rest of your life.

You will experience many discussions and debates with 'I am', but the Free Will choice will always be yours. Sometimes, you will make the wrong choice, but you will always be able to change your mind and return. Sometimes, you will make a different choice, and 'I am' may go along with it. In the end, you both learn something and gain by it. Brace yourself, in those moments, 'I am's joy is overwhelming.

Of course, your rational thoughts and ego will try to convince you that your rational thoughts and ego are your only reality and freedom of will. Choose your rational thoughts and ego and you will be bond to all its rules and pseudo-moral laws for the rest of your purposeless life. You will also get to choose to do or not do millions of don't do rules and live in the gray zone. You will live in the modern world where everyone creates their own truth based on whatever lie they want to accept. That's the world that would have you believe that there is more than one truth.

Your Free Will choice is to connect and live in the Love-light or not. With 'I am', you can always come back if you make the wrong choice. All you have to do is connect.

A Meditation Map

Anyone who is ready to start their spiritual journey, by learning this meditation process, can begin here. Meditation is an ancient practice used in different forms in many cultures, from Asia, the Middle East, India, to the American Indians.

In the UPANISHADS (The sacred
scriptures of India) there is an outline of

our spiritual journey:

> Inside your body is a shrine.
> Inside the shrine is a lotus flower.
> Inside the lotus is a tiny space.
> Inside that tiny space lives the
> creator.
> Inside the creator is the Universe.
> Find it, and you will be one with the
> creator and all things.
> Be there, and all things and the
> creator will be one with you.

Meditation begins with silence and
stillness. This is not absolute silence or
perfect stillness, because they don't
naturally exist on this planet. I have
always said I can find silence in an airport.

Granted, it takes a great deal of concentration, but it is possible. In fact, I became so good at it, my daughter at a very young age started saying to me, "Earth to Daddy, earth to Daddy." when she needed to get my attention. The same is true of stillness.

We need to learn to settle down the body and be aware of everything that is going on within it. All energy needs to flow up through us without being blocked. It is even possible to find inner stillness while walking, running, skiing, or doing any repetitive action.

I usually do a series of yoga stretches before I begin to meditate. This helps me to center my body while preparing to center my inner being. I have seen others use different forms of exercise, from calisthenics to ballet stretches. It is also possible to prepare for meditation while walking your dog. Some even do their meditation during that process.

Remember, meditation is an experience, which only improves with faithful regular practice.

Most experienced meditators set aside one or two periods of 20 minutes or more each day. Then of course there is the Dalai Lama, who seems to maintain a

closeness to his inner being almost
constantly.

Every day, I begin with a yoga
routine and a short five to ten-minute
meditation. This is when I get my
instructions for the day. When I get up,
the 'Great I Am' is already within me.
That is why you hear me say, "I meditate
every minute, every hour of every day."
Every conversation we have is a
meditation. Every time 'I am' asks me to
listen, is a meditation. Every vision
journey, is a meditation with 'I am'.
Sometimes, those vision journeys even
take place while I am sleeping, and I must
get up and write them down. As I write
this, I am taking dictation from 'I am'.
They are not my words. You could say
that this book is the inspired word of the
'Great I Am.' That is why 'I am' calls it a
Bible.

Are you ready to connect with the
'Great I Am' within you? If yes, then this
is the form of meditation you are looking
for. What I offer here will help you get
there. This form of meditation has been
around for over 10,000 years. Devaki, the
mother of Krishna, followed this form
and taught it to her son. The Buddha
ultimately found it. Patanjali taught it to

his disciples. Why it keeps getting lost, I don't have a clue.

The 'Great I Am' says, "It has a lot to do with rational thought's manipulating of the human mind."

Inner Body Meditation

The **first** step in this meditation process is to learn to listen to your natural body. You will learn to shut down your rational thoughts and ego and reconnect to your body, which never lies to you.

Every part of your body is talking to you from your feet to the top of your head. You need to become aware of every part, every ache or every pain. What is your body telling you? Do you enjoy the feeling? Does it want you to make some adjustments? Be aware of what it is saying to you.

Are you aware that many of your body proportions are inter related? For example, hold your thumb next to your first finger. Note the distance from the end of your thumb to the end of your first finger. That distance is exactly the same as the length of your nose. Test it. Put the tip of your first finger in the notch above your nose. The tip of your thumb will now be on the end of your nose.

Are you aware that many things your body does are in your DNA? These will help you connect to your body in meditation. They will also help you shut down your brain chatter. You will become aware that your body is communicating without words.

You will become aware of how your body feels. You will tap into your body center. You will experience the energy moving through your body. This is your body's center connecting with the essence of being within all things. Your body center is your essence of being. You will feel your ego become quiet, because it is completely outside your body center. You will discover that your rational thought has no function here.

You will learn that the body has developed bad habits and how to correct them.

You will learn that your body will not lie to you.

You will rediscover your natural body structure.

You will learn to center your body and maintain that inner center as you walk, run and leap in the air.

Your centered body is the foundation of your meditation process.

Now you can start the Audio disk. And, I will talk you through your inner body meditation on "**Audio One – Listening to Your Body**."

When you are mastering this step and can hear/feel your body talking to you, you are ready to take the next step.

Natural Breathing Meditation

Now let's turn to your natural breathing. It will help lead you to your essence of being. Your body already knows how to breath. It does it all by itself. However, your rational thoughts and ego are constantly drawing your focus away from your natural breathing process. They do this because they don't want you to discover the one secret that will shut down your rational thoughts and ego and take away their control over you and your body.

Always avoid using the forced breathing used by athletes, military leaders and doctors. How many times have you heard them say, "Take a deep breath." Then you puff up your chest and take what you <u>think</u> is a deep breath.

The practice of focusing on your natural breathing, I describe here in detail.

Trained actors, deep sea divers and mountain climbers use the natural breathing of the body. Tell yourself, "Blow out all your air until you cannot blow out any more and then relax." Then be aware that the body takes a deep breath all by itself.

To experience this, place your hands on your upper abdomen just below the ribcage, and relax. Soon you will notice that your hands are moving out on the inhale and in on the exhale. Without knowing it, you do this every night when you go to bed. Try it tonight when you go to bed.

In the next Audio Tutorial, you will learn and experience how this works. This has been part of humanity and all living creatures since the beginning of time. Your rational thoughts and ego do not want you to discover this. Because, they have absolutely no control over it. Not even you cannot stop this from happening.

You will become aware of and experience what the body is doing, how it feels, and note that the rational thoughts and ego are not doing any of it.

In this step, you will discover that your breath and body are completely shutting down your rational thoughts and ego. As a result, your body and you end up with absolute control.

Now, let's discover your essence of being. Put on the Audio disk, and I will talk you through your breathing meditation on "**Audio Two – Natural Breathing.**"

Connecting Through Meditation

Yes, some may connect to the 'Great I Am' within them without using meditation. Yet very few can maintain that connection without meditation. Your rational thoughts and ego are always present to see that you don't stay connected. The result is that your brief encounter will become a myth or fantasy, and your rational thoughts will convince you it was delusional.

On the other hand, there are many who meditate, practice yoga or train in the martial arts and never connect to the 'Great I Am' within themselves. These people usually achieve some form of inner peace and personal comfort. In many cases, they have an improved sense of awareness while practicing their discipline. However, the minute they go out into the world their rational thoughts and ego take over.

Still others may live in the Now and manage some control over their rational thoughts and ego. They may even manage to live with a heightened sense of awareness and manage to accept life's trials and tribulations. However, these people still allow their rational thoughts and ego to demonize their negative emotions and natural pain. That action prevents them from finding their true life's purpose from the 'Great I Am' within.

Even though you may be in one of these three groups or outside the process altogether, you can still learn this meditation process. Then you will be able to take step three.

Now that you are comfortable with steps one and two, this is what you accomplished. You can go inside your body and listen to what it is telling you. You can use your breath to help center your body. You can shut down your rational thoughts and ego. You are embracing your inner peace. You are ready to take step three. You are ready to find the 'Great I Am' within you. You are ready to be part of 'I am's Love-light.

When you find the 'Great I Am'

within you, you will have the choice to surrender to 'I am', and find your purpose in life. You will be one with your purpose. You will be one with 'I am'. You will be one with all others. You will be one with every creature on the planet. You will be in control of the destructive cycle of your rational thoughts and ego forever. You will forever change the planet. Ultimately, you will help bring the Devine Mother back to the Love-light.

I recommend that you revisit Audio One and Two. Then move directly into, **"Audio Three – Connecting with the Great I Am."**

CHAPTER 10
Group Meditation

Group meditation is a wonderful experience. Although, it cannot replace our daily practice of meditation, it can add a sense of community which is greatly needed in our technological and media dominated world. How often the group meets is up to its members. The size of the group can be from 5 to 30 members. If a group should grow larger than 30, they can simply split into two or more groups.

The greatest advantage of limiting the group size to 30 is the discovery of new leaders. These potential leaders will emerge all by themselves with the help of the 'Great I Am' within.

What form of meditation an individual is using should be of no concern to the group. Each individual uses her or his personal process of meditation. That means all their goals may be different. Only some will be connecting to the 'Great I Am' within. It is important to avoid making this an issue. Also, any religious affiliation or lack thereof should not be of any concern. There are many agnostic or atheistic people who are searching for a spiritual direction in life and are turning to meditation.

Avoid the use of verbal chanting in group meditation. Charlatans use this form as a mind control technique. The purpose of verbal chanting is to dominate the inner being, not free it, and it is not a true form of meditation, any more than plan song or chanted prayers can be considered meditation. Avoid it.

The only common interest that holds the group together is the desire to find one's spiritual center, inner being, or start a spiritual journey. The group should be non-institutional, and unaffiliated with any institution.

The location should be a neutral meeting place or a home. The purpose of the group is to be a supportive community to each other, and not some supper movement driven by a cult of personality. When you are connected to the 'Great I Am' in yourself, you will realize that you are automatically connected to the 'Great I Am' in everyone and everything else. My greatest joy is the random meeting of those who are connected. And when one percent of the population becomes connected in meditation the world will change all by itself.

The following is a summary of the format I recommend.

1. **The Gathering (30 minutes)** – Ideally this is in an outer room or space where people can come together, catch-up on personal news, meet new people, and create the atmosphere of peace, harmony and friendship.

2. **Transition to the inner room (five minutes)** – This room should create an atmosphere of silence and stillness and have the feeling of peace and harmony. Arrange the sittables and/or mats in a circle, with a small low table in the center. Appropriate to the theme and metaphor for each meeting, the table may contain an object, a bowl of water, flowers or nothing at all. If people regularly use this room for meditation it will automatically become a sacred space.

3. **A talk or story (10 to 15 minutes)** – The leader should tell an inspirational story like those in

STORIES FOR YOUR SPIRIT. Remember the purpose here is to calm down everybody's rational thoughts and ego in preparation for meditation and not to fire them up or give them things to ponder.

4. **Meditation (30 minutes)** – Open this period with a drum beat, a Tibetan gong, or the ringing of a bell. This signals the beginning of the uninterrupted silence and stillness. At the end of the period the leader repeats the sound three times, with a few seconds between each sound. This signals the end of meditations, and everyone should wait patiently for everyone else to come out of their meditation. This is a wonderful time to observe the effects of the meditation on others. Some may be literally glowing. The depth of their meditation will determine the length of this period.

5. **Conversation** – The leader can serve simple refreshments during the discussion. Allow this to go in whatever direction it wants to go.

There may be something triggered by the story or talk. Someone may have an experience they want to share. One or more persons may have a meditation question or problem and need help. Keep the discussion as informal as possible. The important thing here is to let it go as long as it needs to go.

I use this format in starting groups in different locations. The one question that is frequently asked is, "Why do we need to be as many as 5 persons to start?"

Yes, I know that Matthew 18:20 says "two or three…." However, Joshua is not asking us to form "churches" here. He is already present in our spiritual center or 'Great I Am' center. Here, he is talking about connecting your 'Great I Am' center with that of others.

My experience is that when I meditate with one other person, that connection is very intimate on a deeply personal spiritual plane. Meditation with two to four persons is deeply personal and very private. Either of these is very desirable for partners, family, or close friends, but a different kind of social interaction than that of group dynamics.

With five people, all the principals of group dynamics kick in. The most basic principal of a meditation group is that everyone has a goal of finding inner peace, nirvana, or their 'Great I Am' center.

A group larger than 30 changes in its group dynamics. Any larger and the group starts to see itself as an institution or even a church. Once that happens the 'Great I Am' gets lost in the shuffle, because institutions require organization. The rational thoughts and egos of the members take over, and they forget their goal and 'I am'. To quote the 'Great I Am,' "The last thing this planet needs is another church, or another religion!"

My greatest excitement comes from the discovery that the 'Great I am' is revealed differently to everyone. Early on, I believed I would have to meet everyone everywhere to know the whole 'Great I am.' Now I realize that the whole 'Great I Am' is in each of us. The differences are in who we are, not in who 'I am' is. Embracing those differences is what makes life interesting and creates a profound feeling of unity.

Even though it is important to avoid any dos and don'ts for the discussion, there are two behavior modifications that

I recommend as guidelines.

One – learn to listen to what others are saying. Listen so intently that you can repeat back what the other person said so they can confirm that you heard them correctly. This has three positive effects: it helps the other person to clarify what they are saying; it helps you to understand them clearly; and it defuses most negative reactions. When you have done this, now you can say you understand what they said or presume to disagree. This small detail will allow two people to have two different points of view with total understanding between them. Such differences have made my life more interesting and produced my most lasting friendships.

Two – Only one person should be angry at a time. This has a very calming effect on a group. If someone bursts out in anger and their words inflame you, you are required to cool it and hear them out. The result is that you will listen and perhaps better understand where they are coming from. It prevents your ego from goading you into saying something you will regret later. It also prevents the angry person from continuing to be angry when someone responds negatively to their point of view.

These two behavior modifications will allow you to maintain your spiritual center during the discussion period. They also help create a healthy perspective on differences. And, you will discover that they are excellent at defusing any argument.

The following guideline is very important for any group leader. The success of your group meditation may hang in the balance.

If you encounter a person who is attending for the sole purpose of disrupting the group, and I have, have the good sense to invite them to leave at once. In the beginning, I thought I could convert such people, only to have them feed on the weaker people in the group and ultimately destroy their longing to connect with their spiritual center. The purpose of the group is not evangelism, it is to provide a safe place for people to meditate in silence and stillness and hopefully find their 'Great I Am' center together. The conversation period is there so we can share our experiences and strengthen our spiritual centers, our inner being.

You should avoid any evangelism or conversion.

A natural attraction that seems to happen, because those in their 'Great I Am' center attract other people strongly. You will discover this to be true when your group quickly grows to 30 and you need to form two groups.

THE BEGINNING

For many, this meditation process takes many years to overcome the obstacles and break through. Among these are Zarathustra, the Buddha and Muhammad. Zarathustra lived in seclusion in a cave for many years. It took the Buddha 49 years to make the connection. Muhammad also lived in a cave and finally connected when he was 40.

For most people, who discover this meditation process, it takes several months, or even a year of daily dedicated meditation to break through and connect. For them, however, maintaining of the connection is easy.

A few break through and connect quickly. For some reason, these people have a predisposition to making the connection. Some connect at a very early age, like Samuel, but then need to learn this meditation process to maintain the connection. In these cases, the older a person becomes the more active the rational thoughts and ego become. Without this process, they can easily lose their connection with the 'Great I Am' within.

It doesn't matter which of these tree groups you are in. What matters is that you remain steadfast and determined in the meditation process. You need to devote a minimum of 20 minutes a day to meditation. Only then do you have any chance of shutting down your rational thoughts and ego. Then you will be able to make your connection with the 'Great I Am' within you a lasting one.

Once, I had a student, Johnathan, in one of my classes. The class was filled to capacity with 30 students. The first two sessions were a bit noisy, and everyone was having a tough time settling down and getting into the meditation process.

I could see from day one that Johnathan's annoyance with the others in the class is getting the best of him. On the third day, Johnathan listens carefully to the instructions and then disappeared into the stairwell that leads down to the emergency exit. I start after him, but the 'Great I Am' tells me to let him be. I just assume that he is leaving, because of issues.

At the next class, Johnathan is present again. Again, he listens to the instructions and exits through the stairwell door. The 'Great I Am's message is the same. The rest of the class is starting to settle down and listen to their bodies in the meditation process.

This goes on for the rest of the week, and 'I am's message is always the same. By the end of the week, I am having no reaction to Johnathan's leaving. The rest of the students pay no attention ether.

On Monday, Johnathan is there. He listens to the instructions and leaves. This time, I barely notice that he is leaving. I immediately jump into helping the others get started, with a little pep talk.

As I finish, the 'Great I Am' is in my ear, "Johnathan needs your help. He is having a crisis."

I look at the exit door.

"Yes, he is out there."

I quickly check the others and head for the exit door.

I open the door and look in awl. Johnathan's mat and gear sit neatly on the landing, including a portable sittable. Finally, I see Johnathan sitting on the stairs, with his head in his hands.

As I cross to him, the 'Great I Am' fills me in on what he has been doing in setting up his own private little space.

I sit down and ask, "Can I help?"

Johnathan mumbles into his hands, "No one can help! I am a junky and a pot head. You said we had to be drug free to do this. So, last week, I went cold turkey. It was cool until Saturday and Sunday. Then, my rational brain chatter is on constantly. I end up with the shakes, and my friends try to help by giving me a joint. Now, I come in to start and my body starts screaming at me, 'Feed Me!' I know it doesn't want food, but I can't shut it down."

He sobs into his hands.

I put my hand on his shoulder, "Do you want me to help you?"

"Can you?" He asks.

"Yes, but you need to want it really bad."

"Oh, I want it, in the worst way," he says in a desperate tone of voice.

A sense of compassion fills me, and I know that it is the 'I am'. "Lie on your back and relax."

He quickly lies down on his mat. I crouch down next to him. I continue, "Put your hands on your abdomen below your ribcage. Feel your breath going in and out. Every time it goes out count it to yourself." I watch for a minute. "OK, keep counting until your rational thoughts and ego start to work on you again. Note the number and tell them 'buy, buy' or 'toodle oo' or something. Then start counting again." I watch him for a minute, studying his body functions.

I then tell him, "I'll be back in a few minutes." I go in and check on the rest of the group.

The rest of the class stalled, in my absence. I get them started again and back into their inner bodies. They are now exploring their legs.

During the pauses, I slip out to help Johnathan. I ask, "How high are you now?" We both laugh at the double meaning. I add, "The counting of course."

"I am now on 107. It is getting easier." He seems much calmer now.

I continue, "Good, now I want you to start discussing this problem with your body. Start with your feet and legs. Tell them what happened and then listen to what they are saying to you. If your rational thoughts and ego try to sneak back in, let your body kiss them off. Listen to how it does it."

In a few seconds, he is back into it, and I slip out to the rest of the class.

This is the way it goes for the rest of

the class that day.

As the class progresses slowly through the meditation process, I keep track of Johnathan on the back landing. Like many in the class, he has his ups and downs and prefers to work in his own privet little cave. Whenever he gets stuck, I help him focus to break through. The natural breathing seems to help him more than anything else.

I have everyone walk around the room focusing on their inner center, I check on Johnathan. He is walking up and down the stairs.

Many in the class need to start and stop. I help each person to keep focused. This leads to the running and jumping. Even the best in the class bog down at this point. Their rational thoughts and ego seem to be making them think this is an impossible task. I counter their grumbling with positive tips, with very little success.

Then I realize I have not checked on Johnathan for a while. I go out on the landing, but he is not there. I call down the stairs, but there is no answer. I run down the three flights of stairs to the emergency exit. He is not there. I glance out the window in the door at the snow drift outside. I turn to climb back up the stairs.

The 'Great I Am' says to me, "Look again."

I go back to the window in the door and look out. There in the snow are a set of foot prints. Johnathan is in his bare feet. They go off into the deep woods behind the building and disappear.

I run up the stairs and bust into the classroom. Their doubts and grumbling come to a screeching halt, as I inform them that Johnathan is missing and appears to have run out barefoot through the snow. They gasp just at the thought. That's it. The thoughts. We are all caught up in our thoughts.

I ask the class to get back in their meditation and help me shut down the rational thoughts and ego that are trying to dominate this crisis. They all rise to the occasion and start meditating.

I excuse myself to make a call to security.

When I return, everyone is lying down deep in meditation. They are now focusing and aware. I get them up and pickup where we left off. I ask them to maintain their awareness and start to walk again. Within seconds, I sense that their rational thoughts are about to take over again. Oh bother…

At that moment, the two front doors fly open and Johnathan comes bounding in the room. He is racing and leaping in the air. His jumps are at least five meters long. He literally looks like he is flying.

The class freezes. They watch Johnathan with amazement as he flies around the room.

With one last giant leap, Johnathan flies and lands in front of the Class. He stretches his hands above his head and proclaims, "THIS IS BETTER THAN DRUGS!"

The story that follows is a wonderful account of how he broke through his rational thoughts and ego, shut them down and connects to the 'Great I Am' within him. He concludes with a shout, "'I am' is, OH SO REAL!"

I walk over to Johnathan and share the Love-light with him. I can see 'I am's radiance beaming from his face.

I turn back to help the rest of the class. Before I can say anything, I see that some are already walking smoothly, while others are starting to run.

The 'Great I Am' says to me, "Johnathan's excitement is only a fraction

of what I am feeling. I have great plans
for him. He will fill his father with
boundless joy."

And that he did! For Johnathan
became a new person. He goes on to be a
Super Star for the 'Great I Am.'

Once you connect to the 'Great I
Am' within you, I say, "Welcome to the
beginning of the rest of your life."

Now, your spiritual journey takes on
a new dimension. Your old life falls away
like dead leaves from an autumn tree. Let
them go, no matter how colorful they
may be. Forgive yourself for all your
mistakes and wrong doings. 'I am' is
forgiving you.

You are connecting.

You are making your "Free Will"
choice.

Your inner body and natural
breathing continue to block your
chattering rational thoughts and ego.
They always will.

With 'I am' you can tackle every
difficulty. 'I am' is always present. 'I
am's Love-light fills your heart, both now
and for all eternity.

Accept that you are like the toddler
learning to walk. Be patient with

yourself. Cherish every moment. Work hard to fulfill your purpose.

You are now one with 'I am', one with yourself, one with your family, one with all others, one with everything on the planet and one with the universe. Help protect them and cherish them.

At the end of every day, I find myself saying, "Thanks for a wonderful day, together, Lord."

Every morning I say, "Good morning Lord. What's the plan for today?"

My greatest wish is that you will grow in 'I am's Love-light and share it with everyone you meet.

Yes, there will be rough patches, and the brain chatter will have a field day, beating you up. This is all it must do to get you off center and fill you with doubts. Two days of this and you can make many mistakes.

A common mistake is to allow your rational thoughts and ego to convince you that you are the I am in the 'Great I Am.' The absurdity of that thought is that you are saying that you are the essence of being in all things.

To dispel this myth, simply see the image of the Tow symbol. When you are in the sea of darkness you take the speck of light within you. The light grows and fills you. You are aware that it is consuming you completely. You become one with the Love-light. The self is now only a tiny black speck in the sea of Light.

It is important to blow this one a kiss. Then get back into your meditation and re-connect. 'I am' will always be there waiting for you.

The 'Great I Am'

We are created to make this
Journey with purpose,
The 'Great I am's purpose.
So, find 'I am' within you
And accept 'I am's purpose for you.
Then you will see
Your life blossom and bloom.

The Natural Order

The sun
The moon cycles
The stars, planets and solar objects
Comets, asteroids and eclipses
The seasons
Spring, Sommer, Fall and Winter
The tide
The natural cycle of life
With all things
The Earth Cycles from
Ice age to ice age.
Yet, WHY is it that,
Only the humans species,
Works against the natural order,
Shortening and destroying the cycle?

Remember, the planet
IS NOT yours.

AUDIO TUTORIAL LINK
(With the Print Book)

This book contains all the introductory material and a detailed description of this unique meditation process. The book and this Audio are meant to be used together.

In the Audio there are three Meditation Classes on three separate tracks:

Audio One – Listening to Your Body
Audio Two – Natural Breathing
Audio Three – Connecting with the Great I Am

The point at which to start each audio class is clearly stated in the text of the book.

It is important that you master each class in this order before you move on to the next level.

Your CODE to down lode the audio is: **MB133A**.

Log on to www.RevitalizingInsight.com.

Sign in and enter the code. Select your audio format and download the audio to your device, free.

The content of this Audio is written and prepared by Richard P. Matthews.

www.ingramcontent.com/pod-product-compliance
Lightning Source LLC
Chambersburg PA
CBHW060052100426
42742CB00014B/2799